Integrating victims in restorative youth justice

Adam Crawford and Tom Burden

Safer Leeds

tackling drugs and crime

Leeds

Youth Offending Service

First published in Great Britain in November 2005 by The Policy Press

The Policy Press
University of Bristol
Fourth Floor, Beacon House
Queen's Road
Bristol BS8 1QU
UK

Tel no +44 (0)117 331 4054
Fax no +44 (0)117 331 4093
E-mail tpp-info@bristol.ac.uk
www.policypress.org.uk

ISBN 1 86134 785 5

British Library Cataloguing in Publication Data
A catalogue record for this report is available from the British Library.

Library of Congress Cataloging-in-Publication Data
A catalog record for this report has been requested.

Cover design by Qube Design Associates, Bristol
Printed in Great Britain by MPG Books, Bodmin

Contents

List of tables, figures and boxes...v

Foreword...vii

Acknowledgements...ix

Summary...x

1 Introduction 1

Youth crime policy 1

The initial pilots and evaluation findings 8

National guidance with regard to victim involvement...................................... 11

Restorative justice... 12

Youth offender panels and restorative justice 14

2 Research aims and methods 21

Research aims... 21

Research methods... 21

Referral order cohort... 22

3 The Youth Offending Service in Leeds 25

Youth offending in Leeds.. 25

The Restorative Justice Team.. 28

The youth offender panel.. 29

Panel members... 32

4 Victims' experiences 37

Numbers of victims.. 37

Victims who did not attend a panel meeting.. 39

Interviews with victims.. 43

5 Young people's experiences 57

Survey of young people 57

Victim involvement 60

Young people who met their victims... 64

6 Contracts and compliance...81

Youth offender contracts... 81

Contractual conditions 82

Compliance... 87

7   **Conclusions**..**91**
Integrating victims in restorative youth justice...91
Involving community volunteers..93
The future of referral orders..94

References...99

List of tables, figures and boxes

Table

1	Length of referral orders in the research period April to September 2004	23
2	The age of recipients of referral orders, April to September 2004	23
3	Offences by age and gender, 2004	26
4	Numbers of offences by ethnicity, 2004	26
5	Main youth offences in Leeds, 2004	26
6	Youth sentencing in Leeds as compared to national data, 2004	27
7	Representativeness of panel volunteers (national and local) and lay magistrates as against census data	34
8	Different services received by victims	38
9	Referral orders with recorded outcomes, April to September 2004	87
10	Referral orders with recorded outcomes, April to September 2004 by gender	88

Figures

1	Young people in custody 1992-2002 (15- to 20-year-olds at 30 June each year)	3
2	British Crime Survey trends in crime and perceptions of young people	4
3	The organisation of referral orders in Leeds YOS	28
4	Opportunities offered to victims (%) (n=34)	40
5	Impact of contact with the YOS on victim (%) (n=28)	41
6	Satisfaction with service from the YOS (n=34)	42
7	Age of young people	57
8	Views on the relative restorativeness/punitiveness of the panel (%)	59
9	Impact of panel/referral order on young person's views (%)	59
10	Impact of referral order on young person's views by victim involvement (% agreed)	60
11	Young person's views on meeting the victim (% agreed)	61
12	Young person's views on meeting the victim (% agreed except for final statement where % disagreed)	62
13	Aspects with the most positive effect upon the young person (n=66)	62
14	Length of initial referral order that reached a successful contract (%)	81
15	Length of extensions to referral orders that reached a contract (%)	81
16	Length including extensions of referral order that reached a successful contract (%)	82

17   Regularity of meetings with YOS workers to discuss activities as set.................83
      down in the initial contract (%)
18   Range of contractual hours of reparation (%)...85
19   Hours of reparation by length of order (including extensions) (%).......................85

Boxes

1   Victim profiles..44
2   Young person profiles..64

Foreword

Referral orders now account for approximately one quarter of all youth court appearances and within the Youth Justice Board we are beginning to think of the arrangement as the jewel in the crown of the youth justice reforms.

More than 5,000 community volunteers have been recruited throughout England and Wales to sit on youth offender panels. In most parts of the country, Youth Offending Team (YOT) managers no longer have to advertise to recruit new members who, in terms of age, sex and ethnicity, are increasingly drawn from all sectors of the community. Word-of-mouth reputation of the positive value of the work is the effective recruiting poster, a practical example of civic renewal. Yet, as the authors of this report point out, there is a delicate balance to be struck between providing volunteers with the training and support that the evidence suggests they want and need, and not so quasi-professionalising their role such that they either displace the vitally important involvement of actual victims, or lose the fresh and fluid approach to reparation and restoration which the non-professional voice is designed to bring.

Both reparation and restorative justice lie at the heart of the referral order process. Yet, confirming earlier research, this report shows that direct victim involvement in panel meetings remains proportionately very low. The advantages and disadvantages of different organisational arrangements to contact and engage victims are discussed, and these merit careful assessment by YOT managers whose teams and other resources vary hugely in size and dispersion from one local authority to another. There can be no blueprint for tackling this issue; it will be a question of designing local horses for local courses.

All the available evidence – in terms of constructive engagement, satisfactory completion of orders and re-offending statistics – suggests that referral orders work. Moreover, when the process is demonstrated to them, sentencers have increasing confidence in the process. However, therein lies a problem. As this report also confirms, many minor offenders are being drawn into the panel process, whose participation is arguably disproportionate. Magistrates, despite having been given the discretion in non-imprisonable cases that they were initially denied and sought, continue to make less use of discharges and fines in favour of referral orders. Many minor young offenders are appearing before the Youth Court who arguably do not need, on any grounds, to be subject to such proceedings.

One way forward may be to carry the lessons of referral orders and community engagement into pre-court interventions better to ensure that the positive benefits of community involvement, victim engagement, reparation and restorative justice are realised without resort to the Youth Court. If this ambition is to be realised, it will be necessary for the Youth Justice Board centrally, and the YOTs locally, better to publicise the character and merits, most of which remain largely unsung, of the referral order process. Adam Crawford and Tom Burden's report should greatly assist that process.

Rod Morgan, Chairman, Youth Justice Board
July 2005

Acknowledgements

We are extremely grateful to all those who agreed to be interviewed for this research and the many victims and young people who completed the various questionnaires. We would particularly like to thank John Clark, Brendan Clarke and Louise Hector for their assistance and support throughout the research. Mike Richardson provided data from the Leeds Youth Offending Service database. Thanks are also due to Jim Hopkinson and Maggie Smith for their comments and insights. We would like to acknowledge the assistance of Jonathan Burnett for inputting the survey and contract data, Pauline Windsor for transcribing many of the interviews, and Susan Flint and Nicky Stick for proofreading the manuscript. Finally, thanks to Mike Hough for his support in the publication of this report and Tim Newburn for his many insights into referral orders and their implementation.

Summary

This research reports the findings of an evaluation of the work of the Restorative Justice Team (RJ Team) within the Leeds Youth Offending Service (YOS) with regard to victim involvement and input into referral orders and youth offender panels. Through an examination of a six-month cohort of cases in 2004, the research draws upon qualitative and quantitative data, including a survey of young people and victims who did not attend panel meetings, as well as in-depth interviews with victims who attended a panel meeting, young people and their parents.

The central findings of the evaluation are that:

- The victim liaison officers (VLOs) and the RJ Team made a significant and valuable impact upon the delivery of referral orders and the organisation of youth offender panels. This work helped integrate victims more centrally within the referral order process, gave them a greater say and helped young people confront the consequences of their offending.
- While important first steps have been taken in integrating a victim perspective into the centre of service delivery, more work remains to be done to increase victim involvement and raise victim awareness, both within the referral order process and in the work of the YOS more generally.
- Youth offender panels provide a constructive and participatory forum in which to address young people's offending behaviour and to deliberate upon reparation to the victim and/or community. Their informal atmosphere and inclusive practice allow young people, their parents or carers, victims (where they attend), community panel members and YOS staff opportunities to discuss the nature and consequences of offending, as well as how to respond to this in ways that seek to repair the harm done and to address the causes of the young person's offending behaviour.

Victims

Involving victims in a meaningful and sensitive way within the youth offender panel process constitutes one of the greatest challenges in realising the full potential of referral orders. The research found that the level of victim attendance at panel meetings remains low by comparative measures. A victim attended an initial panel meeting in less than 9% of eligible cases. National standards, requiring the initial panel meeting to be held within 20 working days of the referral order being issued by the court and victims to be contacted within five working days of that date, often militate against high levels of victim involvement at initial panel meetings.

Good-quality victim liaison work is both time-consuming and labour-intensive. The employment of dedicated VLOs affords a way of ensuring that victims' needs and interests are given due significance within the youth offender panel process and the referral order as a whole.

Specialist VLOs can, and do, act as champions of the victims' perspective within the YOS and ensure that victims are accorded the appropriate role and voice that they deserve and the original legislation intended. However, one unintended consequence of providing dedicated VLOs can be that they may deflect responsibility from other YOS staff and, hence, may do less to transform the culture and workings of the organisation as a whole.

The Leeds YOS made important strides to ensure both that dedicated workers within the RJ Team represent victims' needs and interests, and that a victim perspective is accorded due status throughout the work of the service. Victims who had contact with the service accord to it very high levels of satisfaction.

- The experience illustrates some of the difficulties of identifying victims and, more particularly, in encouraging 'corporate victims' to attend panel meetings.
- The evidence suggests clear thought needs to be given to providing victims with alternative means of input to panel meetings.
- There can be a tension between the requirements of informed consent and the aim of involving as many victims as possible in the referral order process.
- In the absence of significant victim attendance there are obvious concerns that victims' issues are insufficiently represented.
- In some instances, victims are kept informed of progress only when they specifically request this.
- The experience of VLOs underscores the point that victim contact work is labour-intensive and requires significant resources, time, commitment and training.

The work of dedicated VLOs has enabled the YOS to provide a more effective and sensitive service to victims. It has also enabled the service to contact victims by telephone, rather than by letter, which is more personal and informative. It has allowed the service to move away from 'opt in' letters, which earlier research showed to be less effective. It has also allowed victims who attend panel meetings to be thoroughly supported through the process, which victims found to be significantly important in their experience. Victims preferring not to attend a panel meeting now benefit from greater information and feedback as a result of the work of VLOs.

Our survey of victims who did not attend a panel meeting but had contact with the service shows that 85% said that they were satisfied with the service delivered (more than half of these were very satisfied).

Of those victims that had had some kind of additional information or service, but had not attended a panel meeting:

- more than three quarters (77%) agreed that contact with the service had provided them with a chance to have their say;
- half of respondents agreed that the limited contact that they had had with the YOS had helped put the crime behind them;
- nearly half (46%) said that the experience had increased their respect for the criminal justice system;
- some 44% agreed that the experience had been more positive than they had expected;
- just over a fifth (22%) felt that the service had helped them to put their fears about the offence to rest.

Those victims who attended a panel meeting greatly valued the work of the VLOs and most praised their helpfulness and consideration. Almost unanimously, they believed the opportunity to contribute to a panel meeting to have been worthwhile.

Victims who prefer not to attend panel meetings nevertheless derive significant benefit from being kept informed about the resolution of their case and the subsequent work and compliance of the young person(s) concerned.

Young people

The young people surveyed overwhelmingly agreed that the initial panel meeting afforded them an opportunity to express themselves, to be heard and to be involved in the deliberations.

Young people experienced panel meetings as fair and felt they were treated with respect by those who attended. Of those surveyed 97% agreed that they were treated with respect and 96% agreed that the panel members were fair. The vast majority of young people felt that they were listened to and the panel took account of what they said.

Young people found the panel process effective in making them realise the consequences of their actions, encouraging them to take responsibility and to be accountable for what they do. In all, 87% agreed that as a result of the panel meeting they had a clearer idea of how people were affected and 96% agreed that the referral order experience had a crime-preventative effect in helping them to stay out of trouble.

Generally, young people believed that the outcomes of the panel meeting, namely the terms of the contract, were suitable. A total of 86% agreed that the activities in the contract were appropriate and 77% disagreed that the contract was too harsh.

The presence of a victim at a panel meeting appears to have a more significant impact upon young people, notably in terms of their views regarding how people are affected by their actions, keeping out of trouble and their capacity to put the offence behind them. Nevertheless, there are limits to the willingness and capacity of offenders to see victims in a positive light, to repair the harm or to empathise with the victim.

Most young people who met their victim found this experience difficult but helpful and said that it enabled them to realise the consequences of their actions and helped keep them out of trouble.

Contracts

Victim awareness is a frequent element in addressing young people's offending behaviour, as identified in youth offender contracts.

Contractual requirements were largely couched in terms of the regularity of the meetings with YOS workers. More than three quarters (78%) of contracts specified that meetings were to be held either once a fortnight then once a month (the latter usually for the second half of the referral order term) or when required as determined by the YOS worker.

The research found comparatively little direct reparation and limited use of letters of apology. A letter of apology was a compulsory element of reparation in 9% of cases and was included as a voluntary element in a further 3% of contracts. A letter of apology was a significantly more common outcome where there had been some identifiable form of victim involvement. A letter of apology was more likely in relation to referral orders initially made for 12 months. Here, the figures rise to 36% for a letter of apology as a compulsory element and 18% for a letter of apology as a voluntary element of the contract.

Much reparation appeared to relate more clearly to the needs or desires of the young person rather than the nature of the offence or the involvement of the victim. The proportionate number of hours of reparation in relation to referral order length is broadly in line with national Guidance.

The distinction between reparative activities and activities aimed at addressing the young person's offending behaviour is neither self-evident nor clear. This can send confused messages both to victims and offenders about the value and role of reparation within referral orders.

Conclusions

There is a need to acknowledge that there are limitations to victim involvement. Some victims, for very good reasons, will not want to meet their offender and would prefer to leave the process of punishing and reintegrating the offender to professionals. There may be limits on both victims' capacities to see offenders in a positive light and offenders' willingness to repair the harm caused or empathise with the victim. Notable among the reasons for victims' negative judgements of offenders were the offenders not showing remorse and not taking responsibility for what they had done.

Nevertheless, it is also clear that, where sensitively treated, victims have much to benefit from restorative approaches to justice, particularly at an emotional level. Young people also benefit from meeting with, and apologising to, their victims.

Key good practice lessons

- Victims' needs should be accorded due status in arranging the timing and location of panel meetings. Victims should continue to benefit from good preparation where they attend, including being accompanied to meetings.
- Where victims are unable to attend an initial panel meeting, efforts should be made to arrange face-to-face meetings between victims (with their consent) and young offenders as part of reparation activities or at subsequent panel meetings.
- Consideration should be given to involving victims more centrally in contributing to deliberations over the nature of reparation, be this direct reparation or reparation to the wider community. Efforts should be made to increase the amount of direct reparation, including apologies, where appropriate.
- In all instances of victim involvement, no matter how limited, victims should be offered and provided with timely feedback on the outcome of the panel meeting and the young person's compliance with the activities agreed.
- Thought should be given to the use of different ways in which a victim perspective can be introduced into panel meetings, including letters and written or recorded statements by victims.
- Community panel members should continue to be provided with additional training focusing upon managing victim attendance at panel meetings and ensuring a victim perspective is presented.
- There is a need to clarify, for all concerned, distinctions between work that is aimed to address young people's offending behaviour and prevent future

offending, on the one hand, and reparation work, on the other hand. This would benefit both victims and young people involved, so that they are clear on the nature and form of reparation. In so doing, it would send clearer messages about the value and role of particular activities.

- Tracking cases where there have been different levels of victim involvement in the referral order process in order to monitor and evaluate comparative impact, has been hampered by inadequate victim recording systems. In part, this has been constrained by the non user-friendly nature of the existing software and the data protection requirements to keep victim and offender details separate. The YOS needs to put into place appropriate victim recording systems that allow for easy monitoring of victim input into panels and the possible evaluation of such input for offender compliance and re-offending outcomes.

- Efforts should be made to address the lack of public knowledge and understanding about the restorative justice policies employed in the YOS and the operation of youth offender panels in particular. Some consideration should be given to raising the public profile of referral orders, the role of volunteers and victims therein, and the benefits of direct and community reparation schemes. The development of an effective communications strategy might also enhance the recruitment of additional numbers of volunteers serving as community panel members.

- Interventions embodying principles of restorative justice not only reconfigure notions of justice but also displace traditional notions of 'success'. The diverse aims of referral orders and youth offender panels introduce new criteria of success. These extend far beyond the traditional emphasis upon offender reform (as measured by recidivism rates) to include the satisfaction and experience of the various parties involved with regard to both procedural and substantive justice, the impact upon the various parties and the nature of restoration as well as reintegration. These wider outcomes should not be ignored when assessing the impact of interventions such as the work of integrating victims in restorative youth justice.

Introduction

Youth crime policy

Youth crime has long been an enduring focus of anxiety in England and Wales. The history of juvenile justice, since its inception in the early years of the 20th century, has fluctuated between a preoccupation with 'care and welfare' and 'control and punishment'. More recently, these have been overlaid by an ambiguous and volatile dichotomy emphasising, on the one hand, the efficient, cost-effective and rational management of offenders and, on the other hand, the emotive and expressive dimensions of punishment. Despite the 'authoritarian populism' of the Thatcher years (Hall, 1979), the 1980s actually saw a significant and sustained decline in the use of custody for juveniles and an emphasis upon limited intervention and diversion. One element underpinning this change in juvenile justice were practices of multi-agency diversion that saw an expansion in the use of cautioning and an increasingly bifurcated system that distinguished the serious and persistent offenders from the rest. In many senses, the juvenile cautioning policy of the 1980s was one of the criminal justice success stories of the period. Driven largely at the local level, the use of cautions for juvenile offenders increased dramatically over the decade without a subsequent increase in crime.

The 1990s, however, saw a dramatic swing in youth justice policy, notably in the aftermath of the murder, in 1993, of two-year-old Jamie Bulger by two 10-year-old boys and the media frenzy generated by the event and the subsequent trial. This led to a renewed emphasis upon individual responsibility, early intervention and the use of custody. The mood shifted away from a managerialist informed pragmatic politics to one of 'populist punitiveness' (Bottoms, 1995). In this transition, ideas of limited intervention and diversion lost out.

Against this punitive background, the 'New Labour' government that came to power in 1997 did so with the promise of transforming youth justice in England and Wales. Tackling youth crime and disorder was identified as a principal plank of public policy upon which the government's fortunes in office would hinge. The provocatively entitled White Paper *No More Excuses* set the tone for both the 1998 Crime and Disorder Act and the 1999 Youth Justice and Criminal Evidence Act that followed. One of the conceptual linchpins of the 'new youth justice' was to be the principles underlying 'restorative justice', defined as the 3Rs of "restoration, reintegration and responsibility" (Home Office, 1997, pp 31-2):

restoration: young offenders apologising to their victims and making amends for the harm they have done; reintegration: young offenders paying their debt to society, putting their crime behind them and rejoining the law abiding community; and responsibility: young offenders – and their parents – facing the consequences of their offending behaviour and taking responsibility for preventing further offending. (Home Office, 1997, para 9.21)

More recently, the government published a consultation document on restorative justice (Home Office, 2003a), in which it identified restorative interventions as a key means through which to deliver government commitments to "placing victims' need at the centre of the criminal justice system". It declared that restorative justice:

... gives rights to victims and challenges offenders, communities and victims to take part in building a better future. And, by helping citizens resolve conflicts between themselves, it forms a key part of this Government's emphasis on civil renewal, empowering ordinary people to tackle problems at a local level. Restorative justice recognises that crime is not just an offence against the state, but a breaking of trust between people. This recognition can transform how we approach crime and justice. (Home Office, 2003a, p 9, para 1.4)

The 1998 Act paid considerable attention to reforming the youth justice infrastructure by introducing the Youth Justice Board (YJB) to oversee the changes at the national level. The youth justice system was given an overarching aim, "to prevent offending by young people", and a duty on all youth justice agencies to have regard to it. At the local level the legislation established multi-disciplinary Youth Offending Teams (YOTs) to implement and deliver the 'new' youth justice[1]. Since April 2000 every local municipal authority has been required to have a YOT in place. There are now 156 YOTs composed of about 2,500 staff from the different agencies across England and Wales. In 2004 YOTs were renamed Youth Offending Services (YOSs), largely to reflect the fact that each service is made up of a number of specialist teams. Both acronyms are used interchangeably.

Under the 1998 Act cautions were replaced by a system of reprimands and final warnings. The latter trigger interventions, whereas reprimands stand alone as a formal police caution. Together, they act as two sequential levels of tiered response prior to court appearance. Following one reprimand a further offence will lead to a final warning or a charge. Any further offending following a final warning will normally result in a charge being brought. Once an offender has received either a reprimand or final warning, he or she must not be given a second except in limited circumstances. Police forces and YOTs administer final warnings, which, according to the government, are "designed to end repeat cautioning and provide a progressive

---

[1] Each YOT must include a probation officer, a social worker, a police officer, a representative of the local health authority and a person nominated by the chief education officer.

and meaningful response to offending behaviour" and ensure that juveniles who reoffend after a 'warning' are dealt with quickly through the courts (Home Office, 2000, para 1).

The principal restorative work of YOTs under the 1998 Act was through the final warning scheme, reparation orders and action plan orders. Reparation orders are sentences of the court that involve supervised and directed reparation to victims. The Act states that the consent of victim(s) is required before a reparation order can be made. Finally, 'action plan orders' involve an intensive three-month programme of supervised and directed activities for young offenders, which may involve restorative elements, including victim reparation. The YJB subsequently funded some 46 restorative justice projects. Most of these were either at final warning or reparation order stage and took the form of family group conferencing, mediation (direct and indirect), reparation (direct and to the community) and victim awareness.

Yet, despite the rhetorical emphasis upon an 'inclusionary restorative justice', the 'exclusionary punitive' climate has continued to hold significant sway. There has been a dramatic fall in the use of diversion over the last 12 years. The proportion of young people processed for offences who receive a form of pre-court disposal has fallen from about 70% to just over 50%. In court, the use of absolute and conditional discharges (the least punitive sentences) declined from 35% of all disposals to just

Figure 1: Young people in custody 1990-2002 (15- to 20-year-olds at 30 June each year)

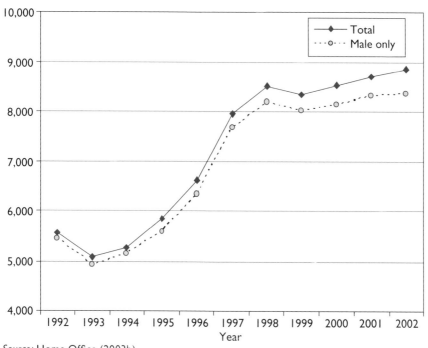

Source: Home Office (2003b)

Figure 2: British Crime Survey trends in crime and perceptions of young people

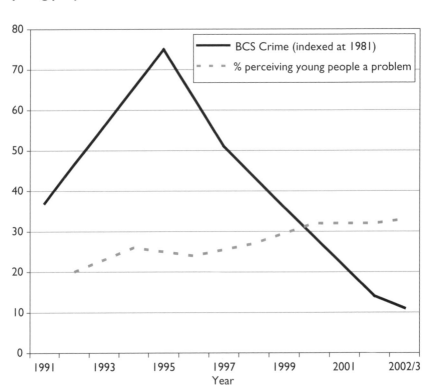

11% in 2002. By contrast, the use of custodial sentences for juveniles, during the same period, rose by about 90%, and the number of 15- to 20-year-olds in custody increased by nearly 75% between 1993 and 2002 (see Figure 1).

Worryingly, this increased resort to youth imprisonment has coincided with a decline in aggregate crime rates. Since 1994/5 both the British Crime Survey (BCS) and recorded police statistics have shown a reversal in the historic rise in crime that has dominated public debate. According to the BCS, the overall crime rate fell by approximately 36% between 1995 and 2003 (Simmons and Dodd, 2003). The risk of victimisation is now estimated to be lower than at any time since 1981. Despite this, BCS data show that the percentage of the public who perceive young people to be a problem has risen over the same period, from a fifth to a third (see Figure 2). Hence, the recent sustained decline in crime has produced no apparent dividend with regard to adults' sentiments about young people. Rather, this reflects something of a schizophrenic attitude towards young people and children whereby their innocence is venerated and revered while, simultaneously, they are demonised as problematic.

The referral order

Against this background, the referral order was introduced by the 1999 Youth Justice and Criminal Evidence Act[2]. This new primary sentencing disposal applies to 10- to 17-year-olds pleading guilty and convicted for the first time by the courts. The disposal involves referring the young offender to a youth offender panel. The intention is that the panel will provide a forum away from the formality of the court where the young offender, his or her family and, where appropriate, the victim can consider the circumstances surrounding the offence(s) and the effect on the victim. The panel will agree a 'contract' with the young offender. The work of youth offender panels is governed by the principles "underlying the concept of restorative justice" (Home Office, 1997).

The referral order is available in the youth court and adult magistrates' courts. It is not available for juveniles with previous convictions. A referral order should not be made where the court considers custody or a hospital order appropriate. Nor will it be given where an absolute discharge is the appropriate disposal. However, in all other cases where the juvenile is convicted for the first time and pleads guilty, a referral order will be the compulsory sentence. There is a discretionary power for the court to make a referral order if a young person pleads guilty to one or more offences and not guilty to other associated offence(s) of which he or she is convicted. The court is required to explain to the offender 'in ordinary language' the effect of the order and the consequences that may follow failure to agree a contract with the panel or a breach of any terms of the contract. Courts may make referral orders for a minimum of three and a maximum of 12 months, depending on the seriousness of the crime (as determined by the court), and must specify the length for which any contract will have effect. Where a referral is ordered for two or more offences, the court will make a referral order for each offence. However, each order will be supervised by the same panel and there can only be one contract. When a referral order is made it constitutes the entire sentence for the offence with which the court is dealing and is not treated as an additional sentence to run alongside others, although the referral order may be accompanied by certain ancillary orders such as orders for costs, compensation, forfeiture of items used in committing an offence, and exclusion from football matches. As such, referral orders substitute for action plan orders, reparation orders and supervision orders.

The legislation extends the statutory responsibility of YOSs to include the recruitment and training of community panel members, administering panel meetings and implementing referral orders. Panels consist of one YOS member and (at least) two community panel members. The Home Office published Guidance on the recruitment and training of community panel members as well as the implementation of referral orders more generally, which supplements the statutory framework (Home Office, 2002). According to the Guidance, youth offender panels

---

[2] Consolidated in the 2000 Powers of Criminal Courts (Sentencing) Act.

are to be chaired by one of the community members. Moreover, one of the stated purposes of having (at least) two community members as part of the panel is to engage local communities in dealing with young offenders. Selection of community panel members is to be based on personal qualities rather than relevant experience and, consequently, the provision of appropriate training is vital. A comprehensive training package, *Panel Matters*, has been developed for this purpose. The intention is that panel meetings should be held in locations as close as possible to where the young person lives and from which the panel members are drawn. The YOS should consider the needs and preferences of victims when selecting the venue for the meeting. The Guidance advises that "in general, venues should be community-based, informal and non-institutional".

According to national standards, the initial panel meeting needs to be held within 20 working days of a referral order being made in court where a victim is involved and within 15 working days where there is no identifiable victim. The YOS is responsible for the preparation of panel meetings. Staff must contact the young offender to conduct or update a risk assessment. They should prepare background reports, obtain court papers and obtain the previous offending history. In cases where there are identifiable victims, they should contact victims to find out whether they want to be involved in the youth offender panel meeting, whether they are prepared to accept any form of reparation and whether they wish to receive feedback. Victims may bring a friend or supporter to panel meetings.

One or both parents of a young offender aged under 16 are expected to attend all panel meetings in all but exceptional cases[3]. The failure of parents or guardians to attend without reasonable excuse may result in contempt proceedings under the 1980 Magistrates' Courts Act (s 63). The court will normally order them to appear. The offender can also nominate an adult to support him or her. It is not intended that legal representatives acting in a professional capacity be included in panel meetings either directly or as an offender's supporter.

The purpose of the panel is "to provide a constructive forum for the young offender to confront the consequences of the crime and agree a programme of meaningful activity to prevent any further offending". To encourage the restorative nature of the process a variety of other people may be invited to attend given panel meetings (although any participation is strictly voluntary), including:

- the victim or a representative of the community at large[4];
- a victim supporter (chosen by the victim and agreed by the panel);

---

[3] The court also has a power to place similar requirements on parents of older offenders where the court deems this appropriate (s.20(1) of the 1999 Act).

[4] Young victims under 16 should be involved only with the agreement of their parents or primary carer, who should be given the opportunity to accompany them.

- an adult supporter of the young person (invited by the offender with the panel's agreement);
- anyone else who the panel considers to be capable of having a 'good influence' on the offender;
- signers and interpreters, who should be provided for any of the participants who require them.

Where there is no direct victim, the panel may wish to invite "someone who can bring a victim perspective" to the meeting, "for example a local business person or an individual who has suffered a similar offence" .

The aim of the initial panel meeting is to devise a 'youth offender contract' and, where the victim chooses to attend, for the victim to meet and talk about the offence with the offender. Negotiations between the panel and offender about the content of the contract should be led by the community panel members. The YOS member's role is to advise on potential activities and to ensure proportionality. Where a young offender fails to attend the panel meeting, the YOS member should try to establish the reason and may rearrange the meeting. If no reason is forthcoming, or the reason given is unacceptable, then the offender should return to court for resentencing.

The contract should always include both reparation to the victim or wider community as appropriate, and a programme of activity designed primarily to prevent further offending. Where possible, it is recommended that reparation should have some relation to the offence itself. The *Guidance* suggests the following length of order and amount of reparation as a yardstick:

Length of order	Hours of reparation
3–4 months	3–9 hours
5–7 months	10–19 hours
8–9 months	20–29 hours

According to the Guidance, "contracts should be negotiated with offenders, not imposed on them". Moreover, offenders, parents and victims "should feel that they have been treated with respect and fairness".

The YOS member should prepare a written agreement of the contract to be signed by the offender, a panel member and parent if relevant. Contracts are to be written in ordinary language and, where appropriate, to be read aloud to the young person to ensure that the contents are fully understood. A copy of the signed contract should be given to the young person and to parents, guardians, victims or anyone else who will be assisting the young person in complying. The contract is a 'two-way agreement', for which the young person should not be penalised as a result of failure on the part of the YOS to make adequate provisions. The consequences of not complying with the order should also be spelt out to the offender. If a contract cannot be agreed at the first meeting, the panel can hold further meetings. However, if no agreement can be reached, or the offender refuses to sign the contract, then he or she will be returned to court for resentencing.

The YOS is responsible for monitoring the contract and is expected to keep a record of the offender's compliance or non-compliance. The panel is expected to hold progress meetings with the offender at least once every three months. The number of progress meetings required will depend on the length of the contract and the level of supervision considered necessary in each case. Additional panel meetings will be held if the offender wishes to vary the terms of the contract or seek to revoke the order, or where the YOS feels that the offender has breached the terms of the contract. Towards the end of the order, the panel will meet to review the offender's compliance with the contract. Once the period of the referral order is successfully completed the offender is no longer considered to have a criminal record under the 1974 Rehabilitation of Offenders Act.

The initial pilots and evaluation findings

Referral orders were piloted from mid-2000 in 11 areas and evaluated by a team of researchers (Newburn et al, 2001a, 2001b, 2002). The evaluation found the following, with particular relevance to the present research:

- Panels received high levels of satisfaction from victims, young people and parents on measures of procedural justice, including being treated fairly and with respect, as well as being given a voice in the process.
- The involvement of victims and in particular their attendance at panel meetings was both lower than originally anticipated and significantly lower than comparative experiences from restorative justice initiatives around the world. A victim attended a panel meeting in only 13% of cases where at least an initial panel meeting was held. In only 28% of appropriate cases was there any form of victim involvement. The higher number of victims attending panel meetings in some pilot areas was in large part due to the higher priority accorded to victim contact.
- More than three quarters (78%) of victims who decided to attend a panel meeting said that the opportunity to express their feelings and speak directly to the offender had been very important in their decision.
- One area of dissatisfaction about the panel process expressed by a significant number of victims concerned the limits to their involvement and participation in the whole panel meeting. Of particular concern was that 70% of victims who did not stay for the entire panel meeting did not receive any information about the content of the eventual contract.
- Half of the victims interviewed who had not attended a panel meeting had not been offered the opportunity to attend. Almost half of these indicated that

they would have attended if they had known about it or had been offered the chance.

- The most common form of reparation was community reparation (42%), followed by written apology (38%), indirect reparation (10%), direct reparation to victim or the payment of compensation (7%), and then various forms of unspecified activity.

The pilot evaluation report concluded:

> One of the most encouraging aspects of the referral order pilots has been the experience of the youth offender panels. Within a relatively short period of time the panels have established themselves as constructive, deliberative and participatory forums in which to address young people's offending behaviour. (Newburn et al, 2002, p 62)

However, victim involvement was identified as the most disappointing aspect of implementation:

> There is a need to foster and enhance a culture within YOTs and throughout their work that embraces and supports the centrality of victim input and participation within the referral order process. (Newburn et al, 2002, p 63)

Furthermore, the report noted that the problems surrounding victim involvement were, in essence, problems of implementation rather than a problem of principle. The research highlighted the pressures caused by the national requirement (in existence for the pilots) to hold initial panel meetings within 15 working days and to do so in a sensitive manner that allowed victims time to reflect upon the options available to them regarding the level or nature of any involvement. As a consequence of the research, the national standard was amended to 20 working days where victims are involved.

The research concluded that the low level of victim participation in referral orders "raises important questions about the cultural and organisational challenges presented by attempts to integrate victims into the heart of criminal justice processes" (Crawford and Newburn, 2003, p 213).

The initial Guidance, first published in early 2000, was revised in the light of the evaluation and practical experience of the eleven pilots (Home Office, 2002). The implementation of referral orders in all 156 YOSs throughout England and Wales began on 1 April 2002. This national roll-out coincided with the publication of the evaluation final report (Newburn et al, 2002).

In the light of national implementation, the Youth Justice Board (YJB) commissioned research into some of the issues raised by the evaluation of the pilot areas. It focused on three main issues:

- the appropriateness of the mandatory use of referral orders for non-recordable and other less serious offences (which might be dealt with in other ways);
- the use of referral orders and their effectiveness in cases where the most serious offences have been committed; and
- the use of referral orders in conjunction with a compensation order.

It found that in the year April 2002 to April 2003, referral orders accounted for nearly one third (29%) of all youth court orders. According to the research, the referral order is often the first response to the young person's offending behaviour, rather than a pre-court diversion; some 54% of referral orders were made in cases where the young person had received no previous reprimand or final warning by the police.

The research made the following recommendations of relevance to this research (YJB, 2003, pp 49-51):

- Alternative sentencing options need to be available for non-imprisonable minor offences, which would mean returning an element of discretion to magistrates.
- Consistent implementation of Home Office/Youth Justice Board Guidance on reprimands and final warnings is required.
- The referral order should remain a mandatory sentence for serious offences.
- Financial compensation to victims should remain a priority task for the magistrates at court.
- Youth offender panel guidance should be reviewed to include detailed guidance for panels on the issue of setting financial compensation as part of the panel contract.
- Referral orders should not be extended to young offenders convicted after a 'not guilty' plea.

With regard to victim attendance, the research concluded:

> It was not easy to balance the needs of the victim, the care and sensitivity required to prepare victims for participation. This was particularly evident in YOTs where there was no dedicated victim liaison officer. (YJB, 2003, p 7)

The imposition of referral orders in 'minor offences', raised as a concern by both the pilot evaluation and the subsequent YJB research, was addressed by regulation changes, implemented in August 2003. The two main outcomes of the regulation changes are:

- "where a person under 18 pleads guilty to an imprisonable offence or offences and to any connected offence or offences, whether or not they are also imprisonable offences, and the other compulsory referral conditions are satisfied, the court is obliged to make a referral order;

- where a person under 18 pleads guilty to a non-imprisonable offence or offences and the compulsory referral conditions would be satisfied if the offence were an imprisonable offence, the court will have discretion to make a referral order or impose a different sentence."[5]

National guidance with regard to victim involvement

The Guidance highlights four key elements of YOS work with regard to youth offender panel process (Home Office, 2002):

(i) assessing offenders and producing reports for youth offender panels;
(ii) engaging with victims, offering them the opportunity to participate, depending on informed consent and risk assessment;
(iii) attending and advising youth offender panels; and
(iv) the case supervisor role, monitoring the compliance of offenders with contracts.

The current evaluation focuses upon the second of these roles, namely victim contact and liaison work, with regard to which the Guidance declares:

> It is essential that youth offending teams facilitate the involvement of all victims. **The involvement of victims must be entirely voluntary and based on informed consent**. Victims may choose to attend a panel meeting, to have their views represented, to submit a statement, to be kept informed, or not to participate in the referral order process in any way. They need clear information about the options they have and time to make up their mind, without pressure. Their decisions must always be respected, including the right to change their mind during the course of the referral order. Whether or not to become involved and the mode of participation is entirely for victims to decide; they must not be subjected to any form of pressure that might, for example, make them feel embarrassed or unhelpful. (Home Office, 2002, p 23).

It suggests that unless the victim has indicated otherwise, the YOS should contact the victim within five working days of the court order. Victims should be provided with clear, unbiased and timely information about the referral order and the options for their involvement or input. There are a variety of ways in which victims who choose not to attend a panel meeting can nevertheless have an input into the process, by:

- having their views represented by the youth offending team member;
- recording a statement to be presented at the panel meeting, describing the effect of the offence and outlining their views on reparation;

---

[5] Cited from the Referral Order (Amendment of Referral Conditions) Regulations 2003 (SI 2003/1605) (in Home Office, 2003c).

- receiving direct reparation or a letter of apology; or
- being kept informed about the terms of the contract agreed and the young person's subsequent compliance.

No direct reparation or letter of apology should be given to a victim without his or her prior consent.

Victims wishing to attend youth offender panel meetings should be asked how best they can be supported and consulted on the time and venue of youth offender panel meetings. They may be accompanied by a friend, relative or anyone else of their choosing, such as a representative of Victim Support, subject to the agreement of the panel. In the case of victims who attend a panel, it will also be important to have an indication prior to the initial panel meeting of what, if any, reparation the victim would welcome.

Victims should also be kept informed on the progress of the case through the referral order process. They should be asked whether they wish to know the results of any reparation to the community, and informed when the reparation is agreed and when it is completed if required.

Restorative justice

Given the diversity of practices subsumed under the restorative justice umbrella, it is notoriously difficult to define. One well-established definition of restorative justice is of a "process whereby the parties with a stake in a particular offence come together to resolve collectively how to deal with the aftermath of the offence and its implications for the future" (Marshall, 1996, p 37). This identifies three central elements in restorative justice: the notion of stakeholder inclusion, the importance of participatory and deliberative processes and the emphasis upon restorative outcomes.

First, the notion of stakeholders seeks to recognise that crime is more than an offence against the state. These 'parties with a stake in an offence' include the victim, and the offender, but also the families and supporters of each, and other members of their respective communities who may be affected or who may be able to contribute to the prevention of future offending. Practical expressions of restorative justice aim to consider the impact on victims and others involved, be they family, friends, peers or members of broader networks of interdependencies. These stakeholders are believed to be more directly affected by given acts of harm than is the state.

Second, there is the importance of participatory and deliberative processes for restorative justice. This emphasises the value of participation, empowerment, communication, dialogue and negotiated agreements. Good communication requires settings conducive to such exchanges, specifically informal environments in which the parties feel comfortable and able to speak for themselves. At the heart of a restorative justice philosophy lies a concern with consensus-building through a problem-solving approach to crime, grounded in local knowledge and capacity. Building consensus usually requires that before the process begins, offenders accept their involvement in and responsibility for the offence. Restorative processes emphasise the importance of offender and victim participation – choice and control – in the process of face-to-face encounters and decision making. One intended consequence is to encourage offenders to be more accountable for their actions and to encourage others to take responsibility for ensuring the successful implementation of any agreement reached. Discussion of the consequences of offences is seen as a more powerful way of communicating their gravity to offenders in a way that brings home their impact on victims (Morris, 2002, p 599). A process that treats people with respect and encourages their empowerment, it is believed, will be more legitimate in the eyes of those participating, and encourage a more general respect for the law and understanding of the consequences of individual actions upon others.

Third, restorative justice holds out for, and appeals to, particular restorative outcomes or resolutions. Repairing the harm caused by the crime to all those directly and indirectly affected is an ultimate aim of restorative interventions. Reparation may be symbolic as well as material. The intention is that outcomes should seek to heal relationships. In practice, restorative outcomes often include apologies, compensation or direct reparation to the victim for the harm, and indirect reparation to the wider community, all of which may take a variety of forms. It is suggested that restorative outcomes should be flexible and party-centred as well as problem-oriented. As such, restorative justice embraces a creative range of potential solutions (as opposed to a list of presumptive sanctions). One of the hopes of restorative justice is that there will be some reconciliation, *rapprochement* or greater mutual understanding between the parties. The reintegration of offenders into the broader community is also a desired outcome.

Van Ness and Strong (1997) identify four core elements of restorative justice that, they argue, can lend themselves to empirical investigation: encounter, reparation, reintegration and participation. The implication is that the more specific restorative practices conform to these criteria, the greater the impact of the interventions is likely to be.

The difficulty for evaluation purposes is that restorative justice not only reconfigures notions of justice, but also displaces traditional notions of 'success'. The diverse aims of restorative justice introduce new criteria of success that extend far beyond the traditional emphasis upon offender reform to include the satisfaction of the various parties involved with regard to both procedural and substantive justice, the impact upon the various parties, and the nature of restoration and reintegration.

Youth offender panels and restorative justice

Youth offender panels draw eclectically from a variety of sources. They borrow explicitly from the experience of the Scottish children's hearings system (Waterhouse et al, 1999) although, unlike children's hearings, panels are located squarely within a penal context as a sentence of the court. They also draw implicitly upon the experience of 'family group conferencing' in New Zealand (Morris et al, 1993; Morris and Maxwell, 2000), and also on the history of victim–offender mediation in England and Wales, the development of caution-plus initiatives in the 1980s, and the practice of 'restorative cautioning' by the Thames Valley Police (Young, 2000; Hoyle et al, 2002). It also draws on the theoretical literature on 'reintegrative shaming' that accompanied 'conferencing'-type developments (Braithwaite, 1989). This theory involves encouraging offenders to experience sentiments of shame in recognising and acknowledging their responsibility for their actions, while allowing them to maintain their dignity and to reintegrate them into the law-abiding community without stigma. Here, victims are central in enabling offenders to confront the consequences of their offending and accepting responsibility. Family, friends and other members of the offender's 'community of care' are seen to be the most potent shaming agents in denouncing the wrongfulness of the act, but also the most important reintegrating agents in supporting and assisting the offender as a worthy and valuable person, beyond his or her momentary status as 'offender' (Braithwaite and Mugford, 1994).

There are several important 'restorative' and 'reintegrative' aspects to panels in that they adopt a conference-type approach to decision making that is intended to be both inclusive and party-centred. As such, they mark a significant shift away from a court-based judicial model in which the parties are represented rather than speak for themselves. In addition, there is considerable emphasis upon both 'restoration' – which should be a part of all contracts – and 'reintegration' of the offender into the wider community. Not only does the panel have the symbolic power to 'sign off' the referral order once it has been discharged successfully, but also this has the effect of purging the offender of the offence (as it is considered 'spent'). In addition, the reintegrative element of referral orders is strengthened by the fact that panel meetings are not merely 'one-off' events, but entail structured meetings over the lifetime of the referral order. As a result, panels meet to review developments as well as support, discuss and, where appropriate, congratulate the offender on progress made. The panel, therefore, is not only a forum for deliberation about the harm and its consequences, but also acts as a means of monitoring contract compliance and championing reintegration (Crawford and Newburn, 2003).

The referral order represents both a particular and a rather peculiar hybrid attempt to integrate restorative justice ideas and values into youth justice practice. It does so in a clearly coercive, penal context that offends cherished restorative ideals of voluntariness. Yet, by establishing an almost mandatory sentence of the court (for young offenders appearing in court for the first time), the referral order delivers a steady supply of cases to youth offender panels. In so doing, the referral order circumvents the fundamental stumbling-block for most restorative justice initiatives, namely the problem of lack of referrals. Unlike most initiatives that deal with very small caseloads and remain peripheral to the coercive system, the referral order moved to centre stage almost overnight. Coercion provided the capacity to move certain restorative values to the very heart of the youth justice system, and the loss of voluntariness was the price paid. Thus, one of the positive lessons for restorative justice may be that, despite the coercive context, and possibly partly as a consequence of it, change in the direction of delivering a more deliberative process can be realised (Crawford and Newburn, 2003).

Restorative justice research findings

As research shows, the implementation of youth offender panels presents a number of fundamental challenges to the culture and organisational practice of youth justice. First, working with victims presents deep-rooted difficulties for YOSs. Integrating victims as people and a victim perspective as a way of working into the core of their services is no easy task, and may appear to sit awkwardly alongside concerns for the young people with whom they work. Presenting victims with real choices over attendance, input and participation often requires adaptations of cultural assumptions and working practices.

One broad lesson for restorative justice from the experience of both panels in England, and similar reparative boards in the US, may be that in practice there can be a tension between community involvement and victim participation (Crawford, 2004). As Karp and Drakulich (2004, p 678) note, their research into reparative boards in Vermont found 'substantial *community involvement* and limited *victim involvement*' (emphasis in original), as did the pilot youth offender panel evaluation. The concern is that involvement of community representatives may serve to dilute or operate at the expense of direct victim input. Community representatives may be felt to be capable of bringing a victim perspective through their own role as indirect or secondary victims of the crime. This expanded notion of victim feeds into restorative justice models of harm, but may serve to limit the involvement of actual victims. This is not to suggest that community involvement will always function in this way, but rather that in a youth justice system that is often found unwilling or reluctant to accord to victims a central stake (Shapland, 2000), community participation can be used as an excuse for victim non-attendance. The low level of victim participation at English panel meetings in the pilot research and Vermont reparative boards raises important questions about the cultural and organisational challenges presented by attempts to integrate victims into the heart of criminal justice processes.

Second, working with volunteers as equal partners in an inclusive process presents real challenges to the way in which professional YOS staff work. In the pilot sites, although making significant progress, panels only uncovered a small part of the potential contribution of volunteers. There is clearly still much more that can be done in relation to their involvement as a broader resource in delivering a form of justice that links panels to the wider communities in which they are located and the latent forms of social control that reside therein. Panels in England potentially suffer the same dichotomy identified by Karp and Drakulich that "competency building is one of the most theoretically exciting but practically disappointing parts of the program" (2004, p 682).

Third, organising youth offender panels presents considerable administrative hurdles that challenge traditional ways of working. Holding panel meetings in the evening and at weekends requires different working patterns; facilitating the attendance of the diverse stakeholders presents difficulties of organisation and timing; and finding appropriate venues challenges the extent to which panels are rooted in local community infrastructures. Moreover, administering panels creatively and flexibly often sits awkwardly within risk-averse professional cultures.

Victim involvement

Traditionally, victims have constituted the 'forgotten party' within criminal justice (Christie, 1977). In this, youth justice has been no different. Despite the more recent political fervour for championing victims, their role within criminal justice processes of deliberation remains marginal. By contrast, the active and voluntary involvement of victims in youth offender panel meetings lies at the heart of the restorative justice potential of referral orders. It enhances the impact of the referral order process on offenders and can be beneficial to the victims themselves. It allows a space in which to respond to the harm and hurt experienced by a victim, address their fears and anxieties and render the young person accountable for the consequences of their actions.

Rationales for victim involvement in panels are:

(1) it offers an appropriate forum in which to consider the views and experience of the victim(s) and allows victims an opportunity to explain how they were affected by the offence and for this to be recognised. As such, it affords to victims a voice and for their harm to be heard;

(2) it forces young offenders to confront the consequences of their offending behaviour and the harm caused and to acknowledge their responsibility for it;

(3) it enables victims to address concerns or questions they may have – such as 'why me?' – by meeting the offender and the offender's family face to face so that they can better understand their attitudes and why the offence occurred and assess the likelihood of it reoccurring; and

(4) it allows for victims to receive some kind of emotional and/or material reparation or make suggestions about community work that can be undertaken as (indirect) reparation for the offence.

It is now well established that many victims appreciate such opportunities (Marshall and Merry, 1990; Umbreit, 1994). Research suggests that victims value opportunities to receive explanations and apologies (Hayes et al, 1998; Morris et al, 1993; Strang et al, 1999; Marshall, 1999).

Comparative restorative justice experiences around the world highlight a number of interesting observations with regard to victim involvement. Morris et al (1993) found that, in the early years of the introduction of family group conferences in New Zealand, despite implementation difficulties, victims attended in 51% of cases in which there was an identifiable victim. Follow-up research into those victims who did not attend revealed that only 6% did not wish to meet their offender. The most common reasons victims did not attend a family group conference were because they were not invited, they were informed after the event, or because the conference was held at a time that was not convenient for them. This indicates that, in New Zealand at least, most victims are willing, and may actively desire, to meet their offender in a forum such as a family group conference. Interestingly, Morris and colleagues note that the majority of victims who did not attend family group conferences were those who were victims of more minor offences (in only 12% of conferences for minor offences were victims present).

The evidence from Australia with regard to victim attendance is even more impressive. In Queensland evaluators found that 77% of conferences took place with victims in attendance (Hayes et al, 1998) and the Reintegrative Shaming Experiments (RISE) initiative in Canberra saw victims attend 73% of conferences held for offences against personal property and 90% for violent incidences (Strang et al, 1999). Evaluation of youth justice conferencing introduced in New South Wales in 1998 (based on the New Zealand model of family group conferencing) reported a 73% victim participation rate (Trimboli, 2000).

However, findings from the UK have traditionally been more disappointing with regard to victim involvement, as highlighted in the research into the work of YOTs in the Crime and Disorder Act pilots in England and Wales (Holdaway et al, 2001). As well as the pilot referral order evaluation, low levels of victim involvement were found in the Thames Valley restorative cautioning evaluation, where only 16% of victims attended (Hoyle et al, 2002). Research by Miers et al (2001) found that victims wanted more information and feedback on cases. Research also indicates that victims benefit from continuity of contact and information (Shapland, 2000).

The high level of *procedural* satisfaction on the part of victims (as well as young people and parents) found in the referral order pilot sites, is in line with findings from other restorative justice initiatives around the world (Strang et al, 1999; Daly and Hayes, 2001). By contrast, the pilot research found relatively less evidence of 'restorativeness', again reflecting the findings of other research, notably Daly's (2001, p 76) in South Australia. However, the RISE project has shown that victims' sense of restorative justice (as measured, for example, by recovery from anger and embarrassment) is higher for those who went to conferences rather than to court (Strang, 2001, 2002).

In New Zealand, Morris et al (1993, p 309) found that victims reported attending family group conferences for a number of reasons. First, they attended because they perceived it to be in their interests to do so: they requested reparation, confronted the offender, related their feelings about what had happened, and ensured that 'things were done properly'. Second, they attended because they wanted to help or support the young person. Third, a small number attended because they believed that victims should attend such meetings in principle, or from curiosity.

Some 60% of victims who attended a conference found it 'helpful, positive, and rewarding' (Morris et al, 1993, p 311), reporting that they came to have a better understanding of why the offence happened, and/or that this was a cathartic experience enabling them to release negative feelings. Victims also reported benefiting from the opportunity to be involved in determining appropriate outcomes and from being able to meet and find out more about the offender and his or her family. However, 25% of victims felt worse following the conference. The principal reasons for this were that they remembered negative feelings relating to the offence; thought that the outcomes were inadequate; perceived a lack of remorse on the part of the offender or due to the extent of the offending. The authors concluded that much victim dissatisfaction may stem from "the lack of adequate briefing for victims about their role... and what they might realistically expect" (Morris et al, 1993, p 315). Clearly, managing victim expectations is a central challenge for victim liaison workers involved in restorative interventions.

Research also highlights that providing victims with an enhanced role in the disposition of their cases may impose new obligations upon them. As the JUSTICE Report on the role of victims in criminal justice (1998, p 110) stated: "The criminal justice system must not place further duties on citizens without meeting its own responsibilities for the consequences of introducing those duties".

Furthermore, victim involvement may raise unrealistic or false expectations of what justice can deliver (Crawford and Enterkin, 2001). Hence, victims can easily be reminded of their secondary status within criminal justice processes where these expectations are not met in practice. In this context, victims may see themselves as a 'prop' in an offender-focused drama. Moreover, victims may actually be, or experience themselves as being, 'used' in the service of rehabilitation or enlisted in the demands of the justice system itself, for example in processing offenders or as information providers.

In addition to recognising these dangers, research warns there is a need to acknowledge that there may be limitations to victim involvement. Daly (2003) sheds important light on the limitations of conferences in Australia, notably with regard to limits on both victims' capacities to see offenders in a positive light and offenders' interests to repair the harm. Notable among the reasons for victims' negative judgements of offenders were the offenders not showing remorse and not taking responsibility for what they had done. Nevertheless, it is also clear that, where sensitively treated, victims have much to benefit from restorative approaches to justice, particularly at an emotional level (Strang, 2002).

Research aims and methods

2

Research aims

This research aimed to evaluate the work of the Restorative Justice Team (RJ Team) within the Leeds Youth Offending Service (YOS) with regard to victim involvement and input into the referral order process and youth offender panels. Specifically the study aimed to provide a qualitative insight into the experiences of victims and young people who participate in the referral order process and to assess the impact of victim input into youth offender panels for young people and victims.

At the core of the evaluation was the examination of the victim involvement in, and input into, all the cases in a six-month cohort. The start date for the cohort was 1 April 2004. By this time, the RJ Team had been in post for a number of months, long enough to have established new ways of working and developed novel procedures.

Research methods

The research employed a variety of quantitative and qualitative methods to gain a range of multi-level data, in order to provide a rich insight into the implementation, experience and impact of victim involvement within referral orders and youth offender panels. The data collected included the following:

- a survey of 103 young offenders;
- a survey of 34 victims who were offered, but declined, the opportunity to attend a panel meeting but who nevertheless had some contact with the YOS, and four victims who attended panel meetings;
- cohort data on young people whose referral order commenced in the six months between 1 April and 30 September 2004, including contracts and data on compliance (up to the end of January 2005);
- in-depth interviews with seven young offenders involved in cases where the victim had had input into the panel process;
- in-depth interviews with the parents of the two young offenders under the age of 16;
- in-depth interviews with seven victims who attended a panel meeting;
- interviews with nine panel members (two individual interviews and one focus group interview);
- interviews with nine YOS staff, including VLOs, administrators and managers;

- observation of a group supervision meeting of community panel members;
- contract and other data on the work of referral orders and youth offender panels.

In addition, monthly meetings were held between research team members and the RJ Team and YOS managers throughout the fieldwork period to coordinate the data collection and discuss emerging issues.

All victims and offenders interviewed for this research were initially contacted by the YOS and asked if they would consent to their contact details being passed to the research team for the purpose of being interviewed about their experiences. Contact was made both by way of letter and a telephone or face-to-face conversation. Victims were initially approached between two weeks and one month after the panel meeting they had attended. Offenders were approached near to the time of their final meeting.

Referral order cohort

Table 1 provides a breakdown of the types of data collected during the cohort periods. The six-month cohort in this evaluation relates to the cases managed by the YOS between 1 April and 30 September 2004. As the referral order begins once the contract is agreed at the first panel meeting, we also include a number of referral orders imposed by the court for the six-month period a month earlier, on the assumption that it takes approximately a month between the court imposing a referral order and the first panel meeting.

In addition, Table 1 shows the numbers of referral orders of different lengths given during the research period. For the purposes of comparison, the final column shows the figures for referral orders of different lengths in the six-month period preceding the beginning of the research.

Table 2 shows the age of recipients of referral orders during the research period. The distribution of referral orders across the relevant age range is very similar to that which occurred in the preceding 18 months.

Table 1: Length of referral orders in the research period April to September 2004

	Male	Female	All	%	% earlier
3 months	71	21	93	43.3	45.3
4 months	29	13	42	19.5	16.3
5 months	2	2	4	1.9	1.9
6 months	37	13	50	23.3	21.9
7 months			0	0.0	0.4
8 months	3	1	4	1.9	3.6
9 months	5	2	7	3.3	6.2
10 months			0	0.0	1.0
11 months			0	0.0	0.0
12 months	10	0	10	4.7	3.5
No information	3	2	5	2.3	
TOTALS			215	100.2	100.1

Note: The figures do not include the extensions given to seven young people (four male and three female). In six of these cases the extension was for three months.

Table 2: The age of recipients of referral orders, April to September 2004

Age	Male	Female	Number	%
10-12	12	3	15	7.0
13	20	4	24	11.2
14	23	10	33	15.3
15	38	12	50	23.3
16	32	13	45	20.9
17	33	13	46	21.4
TOTALS	158	55	213	99.1

3

The Youth Offending Service in Leeds

Youth offending in Leeds

Leeds Youth Offending Service (YOS) operates within a complex statutory, organisational and funding framework. It is managed locally by the YOS Partnership, which includes social services, probation, health, education and police. The YOS is funded by a combination of the Youth Justice Board (YJB), Leeds Community Safety, the Children's Fund and other grant income. YJB funding is conditional on the achievement of various targets. In total the YOS employs some 115 staff.

In line with YOSs around the country, the Leeds YOS is responsible for dealing with most 10- to 17-year-olds who commit an offence, notably through final warnings and court sentences. In addition, the YOS works with young people's parents and carers. The YOS also engages in crime prevention work with young people at risk of offending, but who may not yet have been charged with an offence. Most prevention work is undertaken through Youth Inclusion Programmes (YIPs) and Youth Inclusion and Support Panels (YISPs).

Within the Leeds area, the YOS reported that there were a total of 5,583 offences in 2004 known to have been committed by approximately 2,700 young offenders. Of these, the YOS worked with some 2,318 individuals. This makes Leeds one of the busiest YOSs in the country.

Table 3 below shows the pattern of offending through the age group covered, broken down by gender. It can be seen that males are around four times more likely than females to offend. Offending levels are relatively low at the younger end of the age group. For boys the peak offending age is 16, whereas for girls it is 15.

Table 4 provides a breakdown by ethnicity of youth offenders.

Table 5 outlines the distribution of the offending between the main different offences.

Table 3: Offences by age and gender, 2004

Table 4: Numbers of offences by ethnicity, 2004

Age	Male	Female
10	44	2
11	113	30
12	209	98
13	427	179
14	703	211
15	885	254
16	1,070	222
17	970	161
Total	4,421	1,157

Group	Number	%
White	4,629	85
Mixed	140	3
Asian or Asian British	226	4
Black or black British	460	8
Chinese or other	16	<1
Unknown	144	254
Total	5,615	222

Table 5: Main youth offences in Leeds, 2004

Offence	Number
Theft	918
Violence	840
Motoring	666
Criminal damage	639
Public order	455
Drugs	329
Vehicle theft	296
Domestic burglary	289
Robbery	144

In all, a total of 2,036 young people received court sentences in 2004. Table 6 shows that against the national average there was less use of first-tier sentences and greater use of custody in the Leeds courts. In part, this may reflect the more serious nature of offending in Leeds as compared to the national average. This would seem to be illustrated by the relatively small percentage of referral orders in Leeds for which there is only limited sentencing discretion. Nevertheless, as a high volume sentencing area, Leeds and West Yorkshire, more generally, make consistently above-average use of custody for children and young people.

In the 18-month period from October 2002 to March 2004, 780 referral orders were given, a rate of just over 500 per year. By far the most popular length for a referral order was three months, with the next most popular being six months,

Table 6: Youth sentencing in Leeds as compared to national data, 2004

Sentence	Number	% of total	National (%)
First tier	544	22.6	34.7
Referral order	502	20.9	25.6
Curfew order	411	17.1	3.1
Supervision Order, Community Rehabilitation Order, Community Punishment and Rehabilitation Order	334	13.9	15.5
Custody	251	10.4	6.5
Action Plan Order	125	5.2	4.9
Community Punishment Order	109	4.5	3.1
Attendance Centre order	74	3.1	3.0
Reparation Order	56	2.3	3.5
Total	2,406	100	99.9

Source: YJB (2004, p 53)

followed by four months. Orders of these three lengths made up over 80% of the total number of referral orders given.

Around 80% of the young people receiving referral orders are male and 20% female. The most common age at which referral orders are received is 16 and nearly two-thirds of recipients of referral orders (62%) are aged between 15 and 17. A relatively small proportion of referral order recipients are at the lower end of the eligible age group. Those aged between 10 and 12 receive only 11% of the orders.

Some 286 referral orders were imposed by the courts between 1 March and 30 August 2004. During the six-month period starting on 1 April 2004, the total number of orders for which a panel meeting was held, and which were therefore officially 'commenced', was 211. There were another 95 panel meetings held in which existing orders were reviewed. Some 23 panel meetings involved extensions to an existing order.

There were 39 emergency panel meetings and 174 final reviews during the six-month period commencing 1 April 2004. During this period 75 referral orders resulted in no subsequent panel meetings being held for a variety of reasons, while some 21 orders were revoked due to reoffending and resentencing.

The administrative challenges presented by the volume of panel meetings are enhanced by national standards and key targets set by the YJB. In the year 2003/04 the targets relating to victim involvement and restorative justice were that:

- 75% of victims of all youth crime referred to the YOS should be offered the opportunity to participate in a restorative process;
- 75% of victims participating should be satisfied with the service received.

The Restorative Justice Team

In order to respond to these demands, a Restorative Justice Team (RJ Team), funded by Leeds Community Safety, was established with the express intention to increase victim involvement in the referral order process. The team consisted of a manager, a restorative justice coordinator, a reparation officer, two victim liaison officers (VLOs) and an administrative assistant (see Figure 3).

While the RJ Team has specific responsibility for victim integration and restorative justice, other YOS staff, most specifically the referral order liaison officers, are also required to play a key part in promoting victims' interests and restorative justice principles. The referral order manager is in charge of the full team which is made up of five liaison officers, who work with young people, and the RJ Team. The restorative justice coordinator has overall responsibility for the development and implementation of policy on restorative justice.

Once the order is made, a referral order liaison officer will make arrangements to meet with the young person and his or her parent or carer to conduct a 'report interview'. The officer will interview the young person about the offence and find

Figure 3: The organisation of referral orders in Leeds YOS

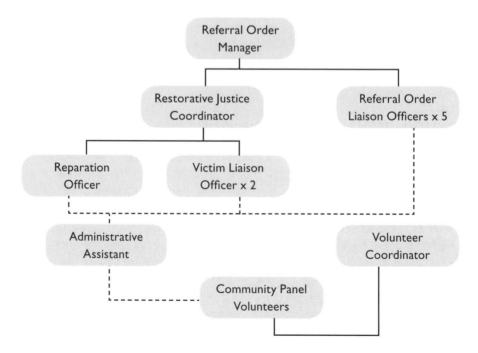

out information about the background of the young person, including education, health, lifestyle, the neighbourhood in which the young person lives or anything that may impact on his or her offending or the risk of reoffending. The officer also explains to the young person about the referral order process.

The main focus of the work of the reparation officer is to identify, negotiate and establish schemes within the community where young people can make amends for their offending through community reparation. When referral orders were first introduced in Leeds in 2002, there were few established community reparation schemes. Providing a suitable diversity of such schemes has required a considerable investment in time and resources.

The task of the victim liaison officer (VLO) is to assist the victim through his or her participation in the restorative justice process. This involves making an initial contact with victims, briefing them about the restorative justice process, assisting victims if they attend a panel or representing their views at the panel if they wish this to be done in their absence, and keeping victims informed, following the panel meeting, about the subsequent progress of the young person.

The role of the volunteer coordinator includes recruiting, training and supervising those who volunteer to assist the YOS in a variety of roles. These can be community members on youth offending panels, but they also include volunteers who act as 'appropriate adults', mentors and for the Intensive Supervision and Surveillance Programme (ISSP). Work with the panels makes up approximately 50% of the total workload of the volunteer coordinator.

The youth offender panel

Setting up a panel

As already implied, there are considerable logistical hurdles associated with the organisation of panels, specifically arranging panel meetings such as to reconcile the availability of the young person, parents, the victim, the volunteer panel members and YOS staff within the specified timeframe. These difficulties are exacerbated when the young person and/or their parents fail to attend an arranged panel meeting. This frustration was noted by staff as occurring all too often.

Finding appropriate informal, community-based venues that are available at suitable times is also a demanding task for managers and administrators. In Leeds, there was a tendency to rely upon YOS offices, although a number of community venues were also used. Unlike some of the YOS in the national pilots (Crawford and Newburn, 2003), there was no resort to the use of police stations. Such venues, while both safe and available 24 hours a day, conflict with the principle of keeping the proceedings as informal and non-stigmatising as possible.

In the selection of an appropriate time and venue, a tension sometimes emerges between the VLO, who may want to arrange a panel around the needs of the victim, and the referral order liaison officer whose priorities are the needs of the young person and/or his or her parents. In the organisation of panels, other interests sometimes emerge. Panel members may wish to see the process through from the initial panel meeting to review. Administrators may wish to try and match up panel members with the composition of particular panels or the attributes of young people or victims. It is often difficult to meet other criteria seen as desirable, for example that the panel members are familiar with the area, or sometimes, that they are familiar with dealing with the kind of offence involved.

To rationalise the selection of panel members, a rota system is used in Leeds whereby volunteers commit themselves to be available at specified times in the future, rather than responding to availability in relation to particular cases.

Data protection and victim contact

A key difficulty faced by the RJ Team in victim liaison work has related to the provision of timely victim contact information. Staff are reliant upon the quality and timeliness of the information provided by the police. The YOS does not have access to the police database on which the details of victims are held for offences where a referral order has been issued. To date, efforts by YOS managers have failed to resolve this issue, which continues to remain a barrier to future progress.

There are also significant problems with data protection. The two key pieces of legislation governing the sharing of information between agencies involved in youth justice are the 1998 Crime and Disorder Act and the 1998 Data Protection Act. As the national evaluation of the YJB's restorative justice projects noted: "One consequence of this legislation has been to affect, adversely in some cases, the ability of project staff to contact victims" (Wilcox, 2004, p 26). It went on to conclude:

> The different interpretations made by police forces of their responsibilities under the Data Protection Act 1998 significantly inhibited the Board's expectations in relation to the development of a victim-centred approach. The impact of the legislation has been to push victim contact onto the police, whereas evidence from local evaluators suggests that this is best left to restorative justice staff. (Wilcox, 2004, p 32)

In Leeds a key difficulty faced by the YOS, and the RJ Team in particular, related to the provision of victim contact information. For the YOS to contact victims within the appropriate timescale, staff were reliant upon the quality and timeliness of the information provided by the police. The research suggests that more could be done through liaison with the police to ensure the YOS either has access to the police database on which the details of victims are held for offences where a referral order has been issued, or is provided with the information more quickly.

Victims are contacted by the police and sent a standard letter inviting them to play some part in how the offender is dealt with, either by writing a letter, by proxy (usually represented by the VLO), or by attending the panel meeting. This letter is sent out after the offender has received the referral order. This is typically around 30 days or more after the offence was committed. Victims are given a telephone call and offered a home visit if they wish. They are often surprised to be contacted. If the need arises they are referred to other services, for example to Victim Support.

The victim may be consulted on the kind of activity that they would like to see the young person undertake. Even where this is not directly related to undoing the harm caused by the offence, it can make sense to the young person to do this because it has been requested by the victim. When victims attend a panel meeting, they are supported by a VLO.

With corporate victims representing large organisations it can be difficult to identify an appropriate person who is willing and able to respond to contact for the YOS but staff on the RJ Team generally reported a positive response from some corporate victims (notably large local retail and shopping outlets) on being invited to take part in dealing with young people involved in offending.

Panel procedure

An important feature of the planning for the panel meeting is ensuring that the victims and the young people are effectively briefed before they attend. These briefings focus on the nature of the proceedings, the people who will be present, the kinds of desirable outcomes, the nature of reparation and the specific needs and requirements of the victim or the young person.

A short report is sent out to the panel members prior to the meeting. A pre-panel meeting allows discussion of any questions arising from the report or issues for which panel members may require clarification. At the meeting there is usually a discussion regarding the kinds of terms that might be suggested for inclusion in the contract and what issues should be discussed with the young person.

Where victims do attend a panel meeting, because of time constraints, the young person may not have be informed about the victim's attendance. It may only be just prior to the meeting when the young person finds out that the victim will be attending. This can significantly heighten tensions at the meeting, and the young person may not feel properly prepared.

Usually, the victim, if present, is given the first opportunity to explain the impact of the offence on him or her. The young person will subsequently have an opportunity to respond. Where the victim is not present but has met or corresponded with the VLO, a report of the victim's views will be presented by the VLO or appropriate panel member to the young person. In this way the VLO is able to recount the impact on the victim and his or her feelings, as well as suggest any possible reparation. Where this has not happened, it is left to panel members to provide a suitable victim perspective.

In Leeds, after discussions about the incident, the harm caused and reparation have concluded, the victim is asked to leave before the panel moves on to discussions about the offender and the appropriate programme of activities to be undertaken by him or her to address his or her offending behaviour, the rationale being that this may involve confidential matters. The victim will later receive information on what the contract includes on issues that directly or indirectly relate to their involvement. On a few occasions, meetings between victims and young people have been arranged to take place after the initial panel meeting, either as a requirement of the contract or more often as part of a referral to mediation or family group conferencing.

Panel members

Recruitment and training of panel members

Given the key role that volunteer panel members play in facilitating the panel process, considerable effort goes into their recruitment and training. Recruiting sufficient panel members is a significant task. Keeping an active cohort of suitably trained volunteers therefore is crucial to the success of referral orders. Key characteristics and skills are identified as good motivation, character, communication skills, understanding and judgement, as well as positive attitude, commitment and reliability. Prospective recruits are expected to commit themselves to the full training course plus ongoing training and supervision, to serve as a panel member approximately 40 times per year and undertake the relevant preparatory work in each case, and to serve for at least one year. Ideally, volunteers will be encouraged to serve for a term of up to three years.

All volunteer panel members are initially assessed for suitability, first at an interview and then during the training programme. The content is largely set by the YJB through its training manual, *Panel Matters*. Leeds YOS provide a 30-hour training course, with one initial full day followed by six evenings spread over three weeks, culminating in a final full day's training. The course has accreditation from the Open College Network. Once panel members commence work they are also encouraged to attend an additional session approximately six weeks later to discuss their initial experiences. In addition, there is a programme of supervision, monitoring and feedback.

Panel members and victim attendance

A significant number of the panel members interviewed had not attended a panel meeting at which a victim was present. Some expressed anxieties about their preparedness for panel meetings involving victims. They felt that they had not yet received sufficient special training in this regard. In interviews, panel members felt that victim attendance sharpened the dynamic of panel meetings for them as facilitators, in a number of ways:

- The meeting could feel awkward or 'uncomfortable';
- It is a very emotional time for the victim, the young person and his or her parent(s);
- In such a context, the parties and panel members can find it harder to express their views;
- But, ultimately, the meeting can be more rewarding for all concerned.

One panel member with significant experience of panel meetings attended by victims commented:

> "It's a positive thing for the victim to be part of it. They do see something is being done rather than that it is being forgotten about. It works better when the victim is there."

The representative role of panel members

A key idea of lay involvement in referral orders is that the members of the panel should somehow represent their local community. However, this raises complex issues regarding both 'representation' and 'community'. The referral order pilots highlighted the practical difficulties of ensuring a representative composition of lay volunteers (Crawford and Newburn, 2002). Research conducted eight months after the national implementation of referral orders suggested that by the end of December 2002 there were 5,130 panel volunteers across England and Wales who had completed training and were sitting on panels, with a further 2,009 people awaiting training (Biermann and Moulton, 2003).[6] The research also found that, despite an over-representation of women (65% of all volunteers), panel members broadly reflected the general population, as against recent census data (Table

---

[6] There are now estimated to be up to 6,000 community panel volunteers across the country.

Table 7: Representativeness of panel volunteers (national and local) and lay magistrates as against census data

	Census 2001 (%)	YOP Volunteers 2002 (%)	Leeds Panel Volunteers 2005 (%)	Lay Magistrates 2001 (%)
Female	52	65	74	49
Under 40	35	37	54	4
60-75	19	12	11	32
Black	2	7	6	2
Asian	4	3	6	3
Other non-white	2	1	13	2
Unemployed	3	3	10	n/a

Source: Adapted from Biermann and Moulton (2003)

7). Certainly, at a national level, panel volunteers are more representative of the population than lay magistrates, particularly with regard to age and ethnic origin.

At the end of March 2005 the Leeds YOS had a total of 80 panel volunteers on its books, although 11 were temporarily 'out of action' for various reasons. In addition, the YOS had a further 16 undergoing initial training. Of the 80 trained panel members 59 were female and 21 male, 43 were under 40 years of age and nine aged 60 or over (see Table 7). In terms of ethnicity, five panel members described themselves as black, another five as Asian and 10 as other non-white. Some 25 were defined as unemployed, of whom seven classified themselves as retired and 10 were students.

Against the national average and census data, the Leeds scheme clearly has a preponderance of women. Staff in Leeds identified this as an issue that they were seeking to address. However, there is a healthy representation of panel members aged under 40 and a strong representation of minority ethnic groups.

Leeds YOS staff, in interview, noted that the lack of public knowledge and understanding about youth offender panels hindered their recruitment drives for volunteers. If was felt that greater public understanding of the work of youth offender panels would help attract new recruits.

Panel members themselves saw their role as simultaneously representing the wider community as the indirect victim of offending and also as an impartial mediator. They articulated the importance of not taking sides. As one panel volunteer said:

"We've got to be in the middle. We can't be seen to be taking sides. We've got to ensure the victim has their say. We don't want to be seen as ganging up on the young person. We have to make sure both sides get some input into it."

Reparation and 'interventions'

Reparation is a required element of all youth offender contracts. This can be either direct to the victim or to the wider community. The former might involve an apology and/or some practical form of redress. Indirect reparation, in theory at least, entails making some form of contribution to the wider community to help repair or make up for the damage done to it by the offence. However, trying to tailor the reparation to the offence and trying to find suitable reparative activities were acknowledged to be extremely difficult tasks. Furthermore, finding adequate supervision for reparative activities was also problematic. The evaluation of the national pilots found that:

> Whether through lack of imaginative ideas or lack of resources, there was a growing tendency in all the pilot areas to use the same reparative activities over and over. One of the dangers with this was that it ran the risk of being incommensurate to the offence, thus diminishing its relevance in the eyes of the offender. (Crawford and Newburn, 2003, p 137)

Whilst, in principle, the relationship between reparation and offence is important both symbolically and instrumentally for the young person, victim and wider community, in reality this association is often less apparent. First, there is an ever-present danger that community reparation is experienced as a form of community service order, particularly given the government's emphasis on Community Payback schemes. Interestingly, in interview a number of young people and their parents erroneously described their reparation activities as 'community service'. Secondly, in practice, it is not always easy to distinguish between reparation and the programme of activities designed to address the young person's offending behaviour. In some cases, for example, as we shall see in the case of the fire service project, the two elements are intimately linked and conflated.

In order to address some of these difficulties the Leeds YOS employed a reparation officer with the explicit task of establishing a range of interventions from which a selection could be made to meet the needs of any particular case or young person. As a result of the investment in the role of the reparation officer, the Leeds YOS was able to build up contacts with a broad variety of community reparation projects. Links with about 48 schemes were established over a three-month period. This included a range of schemes in different areas to ensure geographical spread and a variety of types of projects which could be related to different patterns of offending. Despite this, the YOS continued to expand the number and range of reparation schemes.

4

Victims' experiences

Numbers of victims

In this section we explore the experiences of victims who have been contacted by the Leeds YOS and examine the different options for victim input. According to the data, during the six months between 1 April and 30 September 2004, a total number of 211 referral orders commenced with a first panel meeting. In 64 of these cases no victim was identified. Of the 147 cases in which at least one victim was identified, a victim attended a panel meeting in only 13 cases. This represents an attendance rate of less than 9% of eligible cases.[7] In this period the VLOs in the Leeds YOS identified and contacted some 255 victims. This figure is larger than the number of cases in which a victim was identified, as some cases involved multiple victims. This means that the attendance rate during this period by victim, rather than by case, is even lower. Only 5% of victims contacted actually attended a panel meeting.[8]

Although few victims took up the opportunity to attend a panel meeting, many other victims derived benefit from the victim liaison service in other ways. This is forcefully illustrated by the survey of victims who did not attend a panel meeting (to which we return later).

The cornerstone of restorative justice is that victim involvement should be entirely voluntary. For understandable reasons, victims may choose not to attend a panel meeting or not to contribute in any way to the panel process. Such views must be respected. Nevertheless, there are diverse ways – notably through the provision of documentation and discussion – in which victims can be provided with information and can be facilitated and encouraged to consider attending a panel meeting or making some other form of input or contribution to the process.

There are, arguably, eight crucial steps in the victim contact and consultation process (see Newburn et al, 2001b):

---

[7] This is lower than the average of 13% found in the evaluation of the 11 pilot sites (Newburn et al, 2002).

[8] It is worth noting that some victims who had been contacted in this period may have attended a subsequent panel meeting outside of the focused timeframe. However, the data available suggest that this was unlikely to account for a significant number of victims who subsequently attended a panel meeting.

Table 8: Different services received by victims

	Total number of victims	% of victims provided service
Contacted by telephone by VLO	219	86
Received a home visit	113	52
Had their views presented at a panel by YOS representative	132	60
Provided with long-term support (in excess of six months)	5	2
Attended a panel meeting	13	5

- identifying victims;
- contacting victims;
- providing victims with choices;
- securing victims' consent;
- assessing victims' suitability to attend a panel meeting
- facilitating victim attendance through practical measures;
- victim input at initial panel meetings; and
- follow-up – keeping the victim informed of progress.

At each of these stages, it is important to give due weight to victims' needs, otherwise victims can 'fall between the gaps' of a service primarily organised around young people's needs. From the outset, identifying a victim can be less straightforward than supposed. While in certain cases the existence of a victim will be apparent, in a number of instances ascribing the status of victim is more problematic. Identifying victims depends both upon the quality of the information available about the case and how inclusive or wide-ranging an interpretation of 'victim' is offered. Moreover, the process of identifying victims is largely done before cases and names are referred to the RJ Team, who are therefore, dependent upon the judgements of others.

We can identify a number of specific obstacles to victim involvement:

Administrative pressures of time militate against active encouragement of victim attendance, in particular the 20-day timetable for the initial panel meeting as set by national standards. Despite the support provided by the YOS, particularly VLOs in meeting victims beforehand, attending panels can place an inconvenient burden upon victims. From our survey of those victims who did not attend a panel meeting; some 12% said that they did not do so because they were too busy and another 12% because it was at an inconvenient time or place. Some 3% of respondents saw the offence as relatively minor or trivial and, therefore, not seeming to require such a response. The survey identified this as a reason not to have attended a panel meeting.

Public ignorance about youth offender panels and the workings of referral orders is apparent. As such, convincing victims of the value of attending something that they have little knowledge about can be difficult. The absence of a wider public debate about, and publicity over, the work of youth offender panels has left the considerable task of explaining to victims (who would not otherwise have heard of them) the nature of referral orders to those engaging in initial victim contact work.

Tracking victim involvement in the referral order process in order to monitor and evaluate comparative impact is often hampered by inadequate victim recording systems, partly due to the non-user-friendly nature of the existing YOS software and the data protection requirements to keep victim and offender details separate.

Victims who did not attend a panel meeting

We surveyed all victims who had been contacted by the RJ Team in the Leeds YOS and offered input into the youth offender panel during the research period. We received 34 responses from victims who had not taken up the offer to attend a panel meeting.[9] More than three fifths were female. They represented a broad spectrum of age groups. A third were aged under 20 and another third were between 40 and 59, with a quarter aged between 20 and 39, and the rest over 60. The respondents had been victims of a variety of offences.

Victims were asked to identify up to two main reasons why they did not attend the panel meeting. The three most common reasons, in descending order, were that they preferred to leave it to the professionals (47%), did not want to meet the offender (35%) and feared reprisals (29%).

In three cases the victim had wanted to attend the panel meeting but the young person did not turn up. Clearly the experience of these victims clouded some of their responses (they will be considered separately where appropriate). In one other case the victim's son went to the same school as the offender and this was given as the reason not to attend.

When they were first approached by the YOS and asked if they would like to attend the youth offender panel meeting, most victims felt that they understood the process that they were being invited to get involved in. Nearly all said that they understood the process very or quite well, and more than nine tenths said that they were given the right amount of information about the referral order. All respondents said that they were given the right amount of information about what would happen at the panel meeting. Victims expressed high levels of satisfaction with the manner in which they were initially contacted by the YOS, and the explanations and responses to questions given and the options provided to them.

---

[9] This represents a 34% response rate, as 100 surveys were sent out.

The survey further explored the various options offered to victims (Figure 4). Three fifths said that they were offered the chance to bring someone with them to support them if they had been willing to attend the panel meeting. More than three quarters said that they were asked if they would like to receive information on the outcome of the panel meeting, and nearly nine tenths said they were offered information on what happened to the offender after the panel meeting. Just over half remembered being asked if they would like to receive some kind of reparation, and just under two fifths were asked if they would like to receive an apology.

Victims were asked whether or not they actually received any additional input into or information about the panel process. Three quarters of victims were subsequently given information on what happened to the young person after the panel and more than four fifths were given information on the outcome of the panel meeting.

Only four victims actually wrote a letter to the young person or the panel about the harm caused to them by the offence. Furthermore, only one-tenth of those who requested a letter of apology said that they received such a letter. A fifth of those who requested some kind of reparation said they received it.

Figure 4: Opportunities offered to victims (%) (*n*=34)

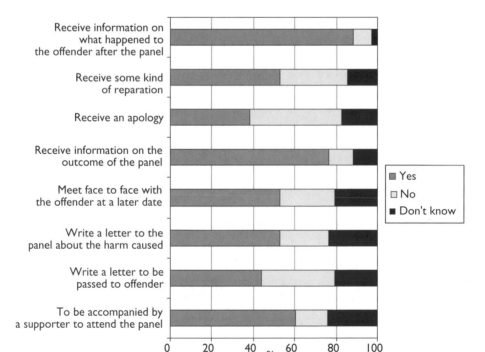

Those victims who received some kind of additional information or service (n=28) were asked whether this had impacted upon their feelings and anxieties in coming to terms with their victimisation (Figure 5). More than three quarters agreed that contact with the service had provided them with a chance to have their say. Half of respondents agreed that the limited contact that they had had with the YOS had helped put the crime behind them, and a third agreed that it had helped make amends for what had happened. Nearly half said that the experience had increased their respect for the criminal justice system and over two-fifths agreed that the experience had been more positive than they had expected. Just over a fifth felt that the service had helped them to put their fears about the offence to rest.

With regard to the victim's views on the possible impact on the young person, just under a third agreed that the young person benefited from the process, as against a fifth who disagreed. More than half agreed that they felt the young person got off lightly, whereas less than a third disagreed. Unsurprisingly, the three victims who had wanted to attend the panel meeting, but the young person had failed to do so, were generally more negative in their views; all strongly disagreed that the young person had benefited from the process.

Just over a quarter of respondents agreed that if they were the victim of a young offender given a referral order in the future they would choose to attend, whereas nearly half disagreed (the rest were uncertain). Victims were then asked if they would have liked to have had greater information or involvement in the process. Approximately a third said that they would have liked more information both about the outcome of the panel meeting and the subsequent progress of the young person.

Figure 5: Impact of contact with the YOS on victim (%) (n=28)

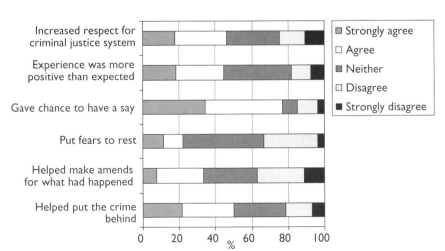

Figure 6: Satisfaction with service from the YOS (*n*=34)

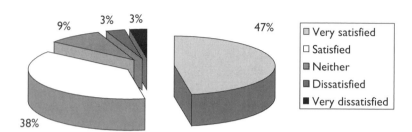

More than a quarter said that they would encourage others to attend if someone they knew told them that they had been invited to a panel meeting as a victim, but more than half were uncertain. Finally, victims were asked how satisfied they were with the service that they received from the YOS and RJ Team. Well over four-fifths said that they were satisfied; over half of these were very satisfied (Figure 6).

Victims were provided with an opportunity to say whether there was anything that the YOS and RJ Team could have done that would have improved their experience. Two of the three victims whose offender had not turned up to the arranged meeting used this opportunity to expand upon their frustrations at not having been able to meet face-to-face with their offender as intended. One commented:

> "It would have helped me now and in the future to have come face to face with the offender to let him know how much this does affect victims and their families."

Only two others suggested areas where the service might have been improved for them. These were:

> "To explain the process more clearly and offer more support to the victim, not the offender."

> "To have got back the things that were stolen or at least to have been compensated and to have been told about what happened to all of the offenders involved, not just the one given a referral order."

In many senses, these comments reflect wider frustrations with the criminal justice system and the treatment of the victim, rather than the service offered by the YOS and RJ Team.

One victim reflected the very positive message from victims regarding the service they received, saying that there was nothing that could be done to improve the service, adding "they behaved impeccably, very pleased".

Finally, victims were given an opportunity to add any further views regarding their experience of contact with the YOS and RJ Team. Three-fifths offered no further comment, and of those who did, these comments were almost unanimously positive. Again, those more critical points made largely related to perceived inadequacies of the criminal justice system more generally, or to the fact that the young person had failed to turn up. One victim, however, felt angered by the outcome in his case, and particularly that the offender would have no criminal record in nine months' time.

In all, nine victims (over a quarter of the total) went to considerable lengths to express their gratitude for the service provided and its positive impact upon them. The following are illustrative of these wider sentiments:

> "I felt it was very helpful… receiving feedback gave me a clearer picture of the perpetrator and the reasons for his actions. It somehow made it seem less personal."

> "I was very impressed by what we learned of the service and the caring and considerate approach of the officer we spoke to. [The VLO] kept us updated as far as her involvement went … My son was helped to cope with what had happened by the officer's friendly, clear and matter-of-fact approach, and by understanding that there is a clear procedure to deal with young offenders. It helped him to put it all in perspective and move on."

Interviews with victims

Given the important place of expressive, emotive and human dynamics within restorative interventions, in this section we provide a qualitative insight into the experiences of victims who attended a youth offender panel meeting as articulated in their own words. In so doing, we draw on interviews conducted with seven victims, supplemented by a survey of four other victims.

The victims

To contextualise the comments and experiences, we provide a brief introduction to the victims and offences for which the referral orders were given (Box 1). We refer to victims and young people by number to preserve confidentiality. To build up a deeper insight, we also interviewed the three young people involved in the offences for the four victims identified as V1 to V4. One young person (YP3) had two separate panel meetings (an initial and an extension meeting) with two different victims. For ease of reference, the young people who met the victims interviewed are given the same number.

Box 1 – Victim profiles

Victim 1 was a vicar whose church suffered 'criminal damage', involving vandalism to the windows of the church hall. According to him, this was one of a series of events that had been going on for some time involving the same group of young people. There were, apparently, three other young people who were not charged, but who were involved in the incidents.

Victim 2 was a woman who suffered theft of mail from her post box. These thefts from her post box had been taking place on a regular basis for some time. Eventually, one of her neighbours installed a video camera and one of the offenders was subsequently arrested.

Victim 3 had her car stolen. She had just bought and collected the car from Manchester, when two days later she was woken up at 1am by the police. A neighbour had witnessed the car being stolen and called the police, who caught the offenders at the scene of the crime.

Victim 4 suffered an 'aggravated TWOC', his vehicle having been taken without consent from outside his house during the night. The car was subsequently seriously damaged.

Victim 5 suffered criminal damage to her car. She had been working at a local pub and had left her car at work one night. When she went to collect it the next day it had been damaged, broken into and there was blood in the car.

Victim 6 had her car stolen along with a mobile phone she had left in the car. The vehicle had been driven and crashed. The offence had taken place at 2am, and the victim was woken by a neighbour who had witnessed the theft. A child's car seat had been thrown out of the vehicle and children's audio tapes in the car had been deliberately damaged.

Victim 7 attended the panel as a representative of a corporate victim. He worked for a supermarket that had suffered shoplifting. In this particular incident the theft involved goods to the value of around £1.

Initial approach

The victims were asked questions about how they were approached by the YOS, their initial feelings on being approached, their views on the quality of the preparation that they received prior to their attendance at the panel meeting, and the extent to which they felt they were properly supported at this initial stage of their involvement.

All the victims felt that the initial approach was satisfactory. Most said that they had not expected to be approached. One victim described her initial feeling on being approached:

> "To be honest I was absolutely amazed. I was so impressed there was such a scheme in existence. I thought this was so fantastic; it's a bit more personal." (V3)

Some victims elaborated upon their reasons for being pleased to have the opportunity to attend a panel meeting: "Delighted really, I wanted to speak to him and tell him how much misery he'd caused and how much money I'd lost" (V5). Another commented: "I was quite pleased, it meant I could put a face to the person who committed the crime." (V6)

Preparation for the panel meeting

All interviewees said that they were provided with help and support before the initial panel meeting. They reported how they were visited by the VLO and then met the VLO again when picked up to be taken to the panel meeting. It was noticeable that victims greatly appreciated having been collected to be taken to the panel meeting.

Victims generally described the panel process as very clear and said that all participants seemed to have been briefed well.

> "The VLO talked me through everything. He rang me quite a lot to make sure I was OK … Help and support was provided. I was visited twice and phoned on more than one occasion. Yes I was prepared … I was very happy with the support which I received. Everything I asked for was done. There was no pressure on me at all." (V2)

The corporate representative said that he was briefly visited and spoken to by a VLO. The time was short because he was so busy. Nevertheless, he said he felt well prepared for the panel meeting and was not surprised by the way that the proceedings operated: "The only thing that surprised me about the proceedings was that they were more informal than I had expected" (V7).

Panel proceedings

Interviewees were asked about when and where the panel meeting took place. They were generally satisfied with the arrangements.

"The timing of the panel was OK. It took place after the anger had settled down a bit. The room was OK. Panel was at six, and the worker picked me up from work and took me there, then took me back so that I could collect my car." (V2)

Victims were made aware of the different kinds of people who would be at the panel meeting and its role. They were generally very happy with the way in which they, and the young people, were introduced at the panel meeting. However, one commented:

"I was a little bit perturbed that they [young person and his parents] were in the room first. I thought it should be the other way round." (V2)

Victims varied in the extent to which they were anxious about the prospect of meeting the young person. Some appeared to be unconcerned while others were very worried about this aspect of attendance at a panel meeting. When asked if she was worried at the idea of meeting the young person, one victim commented: "Slightly, yes, a little bit, I was a bit worried in case he was somebody from the estate" (V6). Another victim remarked:

'I was not worried about meeting him [the young person]. He was only just 13. I was a bit worried about where he might come from. I was told that his parents were all for it (my attending). My main concern was the possibility of getting verbally abused ... I was surprised how young and small he was." (V5)

Others were keen to meet the offender in order to address their own emotions and feelings. For example, one victim wanted: "[to] ask him questions and to look him in the eye" (V4). Another noted:

"I felt sorry for him at the interview. My main feeling was anger. I was worried I might be the victim of revenge." (V2)

For one victim, the anxiety about meeting the offender soon dissipated:

"[The VLO] was so nice and put me at ease so much. I was a bit apprehensive at first. Everyone else in the room was helpful. The only thing I didn't know was how the offender would be towards me." (V3)

By and large, the proceedings were conducted as the victims had been led to expect:

'It was very informal, we all sat round in a circle, relaxed, you felt you could say what you wanted to say.' (V3)

Victims said that they felt able to get their views across at the panel meeting. One described his initial contribution as "a five-minute slot". One victim particularly appreciated the ability to ask questions face to face: "[to] ask why, what gives them the right to do this?" (V4).

Another victim said the thing about the panel meeting which she particularly liked was that everyone had a chance to say something. The victims all felt able to participate as much as they wanted.

Victims were normally asked to leave the panel meeting prior to deliberations about the young person and the interventions that the young person would agree to undertake. We asked victims if they felt that they were being excluded from an important part of the proceedings. However, this did not appear to be an issue, as the following victim explains:

"I wasn't bothered about leaving the panel, I'd said my piece." (V2)

Another victim had her own reasons for being glad of an early exit:

"I left with the lady [the VLO] before they discussed personal things. Yes, I was glad to leave. It was because of his attitude. I was getting increasingly angry with him." (V6)

Perceived behaviour of the young person at the panel meeting

Victims were asked about their views of the behaviour of the young person at the panel meeting. It was apparent from the answers that the victims had made assumptions, or developed expectations, about what the young people would be like, and how they would behave. These expectations were not always fulfilled:

"I had not expected the young person to behave in this way. I expected an 'I didn't give a toss' attitude." (V4)

A minority of victims viewed the behaviour of the young people at the panel meeting in a negative light. In response to a question about whether the young person understood the purpose of reparation, one victim noted:

"This is difficult to answer. He must have had some idea. However, when it was suggested he remove the graffiti as reparation, he said that as he didn't do it, it was not his responsibility." (V1)

One victim added that she felt that the young person was surprised at being asked to apologise, although the other panel members were surprised that he refused to do so. She said the behaviour of the young person at the panel meeting indicated that he understood the purpose of reparation, but was uninterested, uninvolved and couldn't care less.

"To be honest, I thought he might come in and be a little bit embarrassed. The way he was, it really, really surprised me." (V6)

Other victims viewed the behaviour of the young person in a more positive light. For some, this was partly because their expectations were that the young people would be indifferent, surly or unconcerned.

"He behaved well. I imagined he might not care." (V3)

"I hadn't expected him to cry. I expected indifference." (V5)

"He apologised six times. At the end he said 'I am really, really sorry', and he shook hands with me." (V4)

Another victim expressed his view of the behaviour of the offender at the panel as follows:

"It was fairly neutral. I thought he might be more hostile. He's not very communicative. He tends to grunt and not talk. He looked bored. I don't mean that unkindly.'" (V1)

Relations between the victim and the young person's parents

A distinctive feature of the panel system is the role played by a parent, or some other adult who has accompanied the young person. What came out quite clearly from our interviews was the significance of the presence of these adults to the proceedings, and to the experiences of the victims. Sometimes, the accompanying adult was able to reveal features about the young person's circumstances that helped the victim to makes sense of the offending behaviour.

"I wanted to say to the mum, why haven't you got control? The mum was beside herself. His dad had died the year before and he'd gone off the rails." (V3)

Another victim said his view of the young person changed on the basis of the conversation with the young person's brother, who had accompanied him to the panel.

"He explained the background, how the father had died, the young person had gone to a new school ... I didn't even consider why he might have done it. His elder brother explained. His father had died. And the family had had to move. He had got in with the wrong crowd. The lad's got problems. On meeting him and putting questions to him, him talking back to me, I realised he had problems." (V4)

In some cases, most notably those involving younger children, the parent contributed significantly on the young person's behalf:

> "The young person did not say very much. They didn't seem to be taking everything in and me being there wrong-footed him a bit. His father thought he was being led on by another older boy… The father had a fairly key part in the proceedings. He couldn't understand why his child was doing it. The young person was embarrassed." (V2)

Some victims empathised with the accompanying relative, usually the mother, and were able to appreciate the difficulties they faced as a result of the behaviour of the young person.

> "At first I was interested to see what she [the mother] was like. She didn't fit my preconceived idea. I felt quite sorry for her at the end of it. She wanted help; he was a handful." (V3)

Several participants commented on the role played by the young person's mother who was present at the panel. A panel member said:

> "His mum came, she stuck up for him. She could see he had caused a problem. She was embarrassed and a bit upset, and I had the impression she'd wished she'd not been there."

For some victims, the presence of and feelings expressed by the parents helped them:

> "He had the stability of both his parents. His parents were very embarrassed. They thanked me. What she meant was how I'd handled it. If I'd have gone in shouting and screaming, they'd have protected him. He apologised at the end." (V5)

For one victim who already knew the young person and had had a troubled relationship with him, the panel was seen as creating the context for a more considered view.

> "It was just removing him from the situation. The lad is a lad who has caused problems. I saw him more as a human being. It was good." (V1)

However, a couple of victims felt that the young person did not show any remorse, as the following victim explained:

> "He sat with his hands clasped and his head down. When I started talking to him directly he was a bit better. He did have an answer for me." (V2)

Reparation and influence on the outcome

In the preparation for the panel meeting, victims were normally informed about the possibility of reparation and to consider what might be appropriate as this would be discussed at the meeting. Usually the VLO discussed with victims possible reparation options prior to the meeting, as the following victim noted:

> "I was asked if I wanted to suggest reparation. I think the punishment should fit the crime. He was spreading rubbish from the mail which he had stolen. I suggested he do some cleaning up in the area." (V2)

Most victims felt that the reparation was appropriate:

> "I wasn't consulted about reparation prior to the meeting. However, I needed some work done in my garden which I was landscaping.... The amount of reparation provided was right for the hours which were specified. He worked hard while he was there." (V4)

The victims we interviewed held differing views on the extent to which they felt they had been able to influence the outcome of the panel meeting. This occurred, at least in part, because they were generally not at the meeting towards the end when the final outcome was agreed. Some victims were not sure what part they played in determining the contract.

Those victims who felt they had had an influence on the outcome, so far as this would affect the young person, generally expressed the view that this came about through conversations they had with the VLO prior to the panel meeting. One victim explained: "I was asked beforehand and agreed that he should write letters of apology, and continue with his community service" (V6). Another victim was clearly uncertain as to the impact of her comments, saying: "I had the opportunity to say what I thought, but I don't know if they decided anything from what I said" (V3).

Victim's impact on the young person

The interviewees were asked about the impact that they felt they had had on the young person. Several victims identified the importance of their being able to explain the degree of damage that the offence had caused to them. They felt that their presence at the panel meeting gave them the opportunity to do this. For example: "I think attending the panel meeting helped the young person to understand the impact of offence" (VI).

The corporate victim representative's view was that it would be helpful for the young person to have some knowledge of how retailing operated, and of the difficulties caused by shoplifting. Another victim said that he felt that attending had helped the young person understand the impact of crime:

> "I explained the aggravation it had caused, the upset to my wife, the feeling of insecurity at home, and the money it cost. I explained about the insurance, the loss, and the inconvenience." (V4)

A similar sentiment was expressed by another victim, who felt that his influence on the panel had been useful:

> "It was petty, but it was part of a series of events. The lad saw the damage to the church hall as not involving a victim. This was put to him at the meeting. I am the principal victim. I'm the one people come to complain when there is damage. I don't know if the same decision would have been made if I had not been there." (V1)

The corporate victim representative who was asked whether the young person benefited from attending the panel said:

> "He did listen. I had a go at him in the shop when he was caught. I intimidated him and shouted at him. He showed some remorse and apologised. It had an impact. The panel members seemed experienced; the way they handled the meeting." (V7)

It was also possible for the victim to feel that a positive result from the panel meeting was that the parents might have a clear idea about their child's behaviour and seek to help change it:

> "I felt that the main impact which I had was on the father. He seemed to be struggling with the teenager. It might bring it home to him that his son had been behaving badly. He was highly embarrassed and apologetic on his son's behalf." (V2)

One victim felt that the young person understood the purpose of reparation:

> "He seemed very remorseful. I did say: 'I don't want an apology unless you really mean it'." (V3)

However, a few victims did not feel that attendance at the panel meeting caused the young person to understand the impact of the offence. Victim 6 said that she did not think that the requirements of the contract were likely to reduce the young person's risk of reoffending. She did not feel she had much effect on the young person. She thought the young man had an 'attitude problem'.

Other victims were unsure whether the young person benefited from attending the panel or whether the proceedings were in line with their expectations.

"I expected him to be a bit nonchalant, but he sat there and he cried. Me being there put him under pressure. I was very level. I wanted him to know that we'd lost out on trips we'd paid for, visits to clubs, my daughter's dancing, because we didn't have the car." (V5)

When asked about what he thought the impact of attending the panel would be on the young person, one victim responded:

"Impact on the young person? I'd like to think it was possible. I've seen him in the street. I think he's a bit frightened of me. I say 'hello' and I don't get a mouthful. It's often bravado but now he looks a bit sheepish." (V1)

Other victims when asked if they felt they had had an impact on the young person said:

"Yes, I had an impact, it really made an impact on him seeing the person first hand, it was really useful for him. I said, if me coming here means you won't offend again, I'll be happy." (V3)

"I would hope so. The lad ended up in tears." (V4)

"Yes, I definitely had an impact on the child. The parents weren't bad and uncaring people. I told him I thought it might stop him having a life of crime." (V5)

Impact on the victim

Asked whether their view of the young person had changed over the course of the proceedings, victims gave the following responses, alluding both to a shift or change in their perception of the young person and a sense of closure:

"I was a bit more sympathetic at the end. Meeting him caused my view to change. I thought he'd probably been with a bunch of lads; they thought doing it would be a good idea." (V3)

"It was my wife's car, but she did not want to go. My wife was very pleased with what happened. And she felt more secure." (V4)

"It gave me a bit of closure. I was thinking about it for months. He looked older than he was. I had expected a scruffy little Herbert; actually he was dressed in designer sports gear." (V6)

"It was good. I was hopeful and felt positive afterwards. We both felt it went well." (V1)

One victim pointed to an aspect that she had particularly appreciated as a result of having attended:

> "I am hoping it's been closure, but I'm still angry. I understand he needs help and I hope he gets it." (V2)

Victims said that they felt they had been listened to by the VLO and the other panel members, with whom they were impressed. Indeed, the victims generally felt that they had been listened to and respected throughout.

Unmet needs of the victim

Some victims identified aspects of the meeting with which they were less happy, suggesting improvements from their perspective. One suggested that the panel had been too 'relaxed and friendly', commenting that 'it would have been better to have been more authoritarian, more official' (V6).

One victim felt that insufficient regard had been paid to her views:

> "I was quite perturbed after, when the VLO told me what had happened. What I had suggested was that he should give something back to the community. But that didn't happen. They'd basically already decided what to do with him, I think." (V5)

Other comments related to the greater level of follow-up information that they would have liked:

> "The only thing I would have liked to know was what [subsequently] happened? We did talk about what he should do, I'd have liked to know what he had to do to pay for the crime." (V3)

This desire to know more about the young person's compliance with the agreed contract and subsequent behaviour was articulated by several victims:

> "I don't know what effect it will have, I would like to know about what happens to him in the future, whether he goes straight, whether he is still offending or not … My feelings have not changed. But it would be useful to get some feedback on the subsequent situation of the young person." (V2)

Some victims commented upon the apparent limited powers that panels have to impose sanctions on a young person.

> "I was consulted, my gripe with the whole process, and the difficulty became clear, was that the panel had no teeth. I would have liked some graffiti which had been put on the entrance to the church to be removed. We had a wedding coming up.

> People didn't like it. I would have liked to have had it cleared up. It was made clear that there was no power to make him do that." (V1)

This reinforces the finding from research that, where victims are consulted and involved in criminal processes, they have understandably raised expectations that they will be listened to and their views acted upon (Crawford and Enterkin, 2001). It also reinforces the point that youth justice agencies, when engaging with victims, must meet their own responsibilities for the consequences of victim engagement, particularly in keeping them informed with prompt and good-quality information.

Victims' views on increased attendance

Based on their own sentiments, fear of retribution was identified by some victims as a factor possibly inhibiting greater numbers of victims attending panel meetings. One victim implied: "Personally what crosses my mind is, 'what if you see them in the street?'" (V3). Nevertheless, at least one victim felt that more people could be encouraged to attend:

> "By the VLO talking to them, they would know that there would be lots of people there. Normal people, volunteers, and it's not about revenge." (V4)

The corporate representative, when asked whether more victims should be encouraged to attend panel meetings, replied:

> "For minor offences, yes. We do get trivial cases. This would only work for the select few. The parents seemed to care and were willing to learn from the panel. The panel members seemed experienced and carried out the meeting very well and got through to the child and parent." (V7)

In terms of encouraging other victims to attend the panel meeting, other victims commented:

> "Encouraging people by using local publicity. It's about forgiveness. I've mentioned it at the local community association. This lad is a victim too. A lot of people criticise him: 'He's on the estate. He must have something to do with it'. I think it's a very civilising, humanising process." (V1)

> "They should be offered the opportunity; have a good VLO like I did. He didn't force me into anything. It all depends on what kind of crime; if it had been assault it would have been a lot harder." (V5)

Other victims thought that more victims could be encouraged to attend by explaining more about what would happen, how they might be able to stop the young person from offending and by stressing that the panel was not there for revenge. One victim suggested that more people would be encouraged to attend if they heard about the positive experiences of others who had attended and who could say 'it has helped me, it might help you':

> "I do think they should [attend], yes. It gives you a bit of closure. A friend of mine was burgled; they did some quite despicable things. I told her what had happened to me. She would have loved to have been able to do what I did." (V6)

Overall assessment

Finally, victims were asked to give an overall assessment of their experience. One victim felt strongly that the outcome was unsatisfactory (V6). She felt that the panel had too much faith in the young person. She recounted how, a month after the panel meeting, the VLO telephoned her and apologised for the fact that no apology was offered or given. This victim did not think that the young person benefited from attending the panel meeting. She felt that she had been able to make her views clear at the panel meeting but that she did not have much impact on the young person himself.

Most interviewees were very positive about the experience.

> "I found it a very positive experience. There's not been anything that's been negative about it." (V1)

Some interviewees saw the outcome as satisfactory in that they had got justice.

> "It is a good thing, you think you're going to get some form of justice for yourself, It's a good thing for them [young people]. It's a person's car, not just a car that they've stolen. And they can see this … It's a really good idea. Everyone deserves a second chance. If you've been caught, and we've all done it, you deserve a second chance." (V4)

A number of victims said that their experience had been worthwhile.

> "The experience was worthwhile. I'm not sorry I went. I hoped it would help him … I was quite surprised to be asked. I don't like being called a victim. I'd like to know the outcome and what happened after the referral order had finished." (V2)

A sense of closure brought about by the panel meeting was important for at least one victim:

> "This gives a bit of closure. I've been burgled, lost my car, had my car stolen three times; all the other times I felt bad, because I didn't know what happened. It did give me a little bit of closure." (V6)

Young people's experiences

5

This section provides an insight into the experiences and views of young people given a referral order. In particular, it focuses on the impact of victim involvement on young people. It draws upon the findings of questionnaires completed by young offenders at the end of their referral order and in-depth interviews with a small number of young people who had met with their victim at a panel meeting.

Survey of young people

We surveyed young people who completed their referral orders in the period 1 April – 31 September 2004. In total, we received completed surveys from 103 young people, 72% of whom were male. The age composition of respondents at the time of completion of the questionnaire (at the end of their referral order period) is set out in Figure 7.

Young people were asked a number of questions about their views and attitudes towards their experience of the initial panel meeting. These can broadly be subdivided into a number of connected subjects, regarding the young person's experiences of:

- involvement and participation (agency and voice) within the process;
- procedural justice, including fairness and treatment within the process;
- substantive justice, including the fairness and appropriateness of the outcome; and
- restorative versus punitive justice, including the appropriate purpose of the panel meeting and victims' involvement therein.

Figure 7: Age of young people

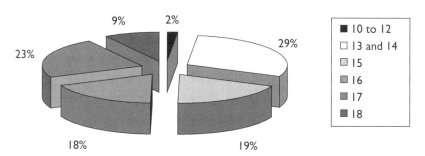

Involvement and participation

The young people overwhelmingly agreed that initial panel meetings afforded them an opportunity to express themselves, to be heard and to be involved in the deliberations. In the vast majority of cases (97%), young people agreed that they understood what was going on at the panel meeting. More than half strongly agreed with this assertion. The overwhelming majority (85%) disagreed that they felt ignored 'in a room full of adults' (again, more than half strongly disagreed). Some 92% agreed that they had the opportunity to explain themselves (just under half strongly agreed). Moreover, 89% agreed that the panel took account of what they said.

Procedural justice

Young people believed that the procedure, as well as giving them the space to speak and be heard, treated them with respect and accorded to standards of fairness. A total of 97% agreed that they were treated with respect and 96% agreed that the panel members were fair.

Substantive justice

Generally, young people believed that the outcomes of the panel meeting, namely the terms of the contract, were appropriate. A total of 77% disagreed that the contract was too harsh, and 86% agreed that the activities in the contract were appropriate.

Restorative versus punitive justice

Young people overwhelmingly agreed that the principal purpose of the panel was to help them; a total of 94% agreed with this statement, most of whom strongly agreed (Figure 8). By contrast, a majority (55%) disagreed that the main purpose of the panel was to punish them. Nevertheless, over a quarter (26%) agreed that they perceived punishment to be a main purpose of the process. While the majority of young people (61%) agreed that victims should always be invited to panel meetings, nearly a fifth (19%) disagreed. Where a young person had had a victim or victim representative attend their panel they were more likely not to disagree.

The survey further explored the restorativeness of the panel by asking young people a number of questions about the extent to which their views and attitudes may have been subsequently shaped by the panel meeting (Figure 9). Young people found the panel process effective in making them realise the consequences of their actions, encouraging them to take responsibility and to be accountable for what

Figure 8: Views on the relative restorativeness/punitiveness of the panel (%)

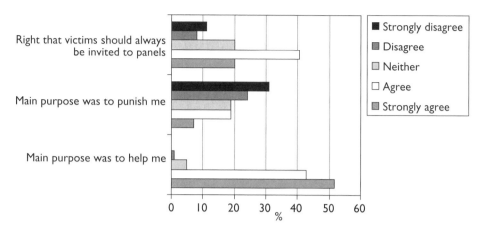

they do. In all, 87% agreed that as a result of the panel meeting they had a clearer idea of how people were affected. Young people also appear to have found the experience re-integrative, in the sense that they felt able to move on with their lives without significant stigma. In total, 91% agreed that as a result of the panel meeting they felt that they could put things behind them. More generally, young people suggested that the referral order experience had a crime-preventative effect in helping them to stay out of trouble; some 96% agreed with this statement (most strongly agreeing) and none disagreed.

Figure 9: Impact of panel/referral order on young person's views (%)

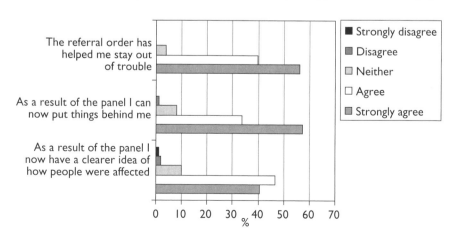

Victim involvement

According to the young people, in only 5% of cases a victim attended the initial panel meeting. In a further 17% of cases a representative of the victim attended. Most probably, this will have been a VLO, but it is not clear whether some young people included the presence of community panel members as constituting a 'victim representative'.

Those youths who attended a panel meeting where a victim was present were more likely to say that the panel meeting had had a beneficial impact. This was not the case with regard to those youths who attended a panel meeting where they believed a victim representative was present (Figure 10). Responses by this group were slightly less favourable than for those where no victim was present. However, these aggregate figures hide a significant ambiguity of response within this group, some agreeing strongly and others disagreeing. This may reflect some of the findings emerging from the Reintegrative Shaming Experiments (RISE) initiative in Canberra, that some victims' representatives or corporate victims may be perceived to be less legitimate by young people because of their status and indirect victimisation. Hence, their involvement may not have the desired beneficial impact upon offenders (Sherman, 2002).

Interestingly, none of those who had met with their victim at a panel meeting agreed that the main purpose of the panel was to punish them, despite the fact that more than a quarter of the other young people (27%) agreed (see Figure 11). They also all disagreed that the contract was too harsh, collectively suggesting that the presence of the victim did not raise the punitive threshold as far as the young people were concerned. Moreover, none of them disagreed that it was right that

Figure 10: Impact of panel/referral order on the young person depending upon the nature of victim involvement (% agreed)

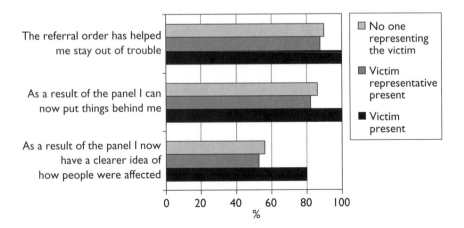

Figure 11: Young person's views on meeting the victim (% agreed)

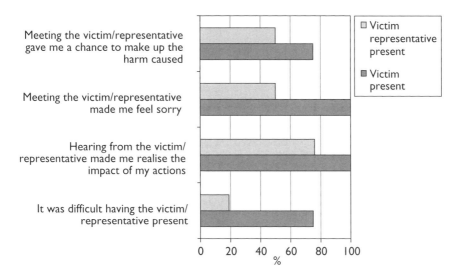

victims should always be invited to panel meetings, suggesting that for these young people the presence of the victim was seen as legitimate.

Young people who had experienced a panel meeting at which a victim or representative was present were asked a number of questions about their experience. Figure 12 shows the percentage of those who agreed with each statement. As before, the responses from the group of young people who said they had attended a panel meeting with a victim representative present were less favourable than for those where the victim in person was present. The small number of young people who met a victim face to face appear to have believed that the experience was restorative, albeit difficult. All of them agreed that hearing from the victim made them realise the impact of their actions and made them feel sorry.

A similar pattern is replicated in relation to other questions highlighted in Figure 13. All those who had met face to face with a victim were glad of the opportunity to explain to the victim and agreed that it was right that the victim attended. Three quarters disagreed that the victim did not listen to or respect them.

Those young people who did not have a victim attend their initial panel meeting expressed a mixed response to ideas of victim involvement in their own panel meetings. While nearly half (46%) agreed that they would have been willing to meet the victim at their panel meeting, 35% disagreed. Similarly, less than half (47%) agreed that they would have liked to have explained themselves to the victim, as against 38% who disagreed. Furthermore, more than half (57%) agreed that they would have liked to have apologised to the victim, whereas more than a quarter (27%) disagreed.

Figure 12: Young person's views on meeting the victim (% agreed except for final statement where % disagreed)

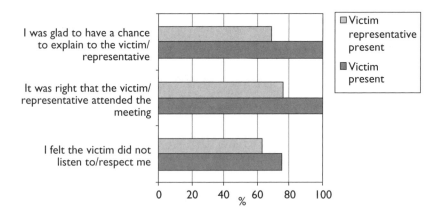

Young people were offered the opportunity to comment on what aspects of the referral order and youth offender panel had the most positive effect upon them, and why. In all, 63% responded. Broadly, the comments can be classified as follows in Figure 13.

Figure 13: Aspects with the most positive effect upon the young person (n=66)

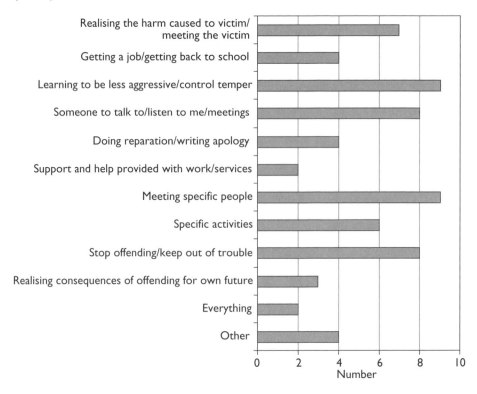

The most frequent response (from nine young people) related to the specific people that youths came into contact with during the panel and referral order activities. A significant number (eight) said that they had learnt to control their anger better as a result of the anger management activities and meetings, while others identified that they had realised the harm caused to victims by hearing from them or about them (seven). Others identified the fact that someone was available to listen to them, or allow them to express themselves, as the most positive effect for them (eight) and the fact that the referral order had kept them out of trouble (eight).

Some respondents went out of their way to praise the quality of the YOS staff and individual workers.

"My worker was so supportive and helped me with everything. I've enjoyed my time at the youth club and plan to do more voluntary work for them." (18-year-old female)

"I think all of the things I did with the YOT were interesting and I took them in a positive way." (17-year-old male)

Others commented upon the open environment in which they felt they could speak and be listened to and supported through encouragement:

"When they speak to me like an adult they understand me. I like my meetings because I can speak to them and let all my feelings out. I like my anger management meetings they help me a lot." (14-year-old female)

"When they talked about how well I was doing and always encouraging me to get sorted that made me proud with what I have been achieving." (16-year-old male)

Finally, young people were asked what they considered to be the worst aspect of the referral order. In all, 46% commented (n=48), four of whom said that there was 'nothing', as the following young person noted: "Nothing bad at all. The process carried out is great" (18-year-old male).

Of the remainder, the most frequent comments related to time and inconvenience of travel to meetings, including having to get up early (10) and the impact upon work or weekly schedules (six). However, even here, respondents continued to be positive, as reflected in the following young person's comment: "Taking my time up but it was kind of worth it" (15-year-old female). Others suggested that getting caught or getting the referral order in the first place was the worst aspect of the referral order experience.

Young people who met their victims

The young people

In order to explore in greater depth the impact of victim involvement on young people through the referral order process, we interviewed seven youths who had had some contact with their victim. In all but one of these cases, the victim attended the young person's initial panel meeting. In the other case, the young person's mother met the victim separately shortly after the first panel meeting. Young people are referred to by number (YP1–YP3 and YP8–YP11) (see Box 2). As mentioned earlier, four victims in relation to young people 1 to 3 were also interviewed. We interviewed a parent (both mothers, P8 and P9) of the two youths aged under 16 (YP8 and YP9).

Box 2 – Young person profiles

Young Person 1
A 16-year-old boy given a three-month referral order (and £30 costs) for criminal damage. Victim 1 was the victim who attended this young person's panel meeting. The young person's mother attended the initial panel meeting. His contract required the following activities:

> To address offending behaviour; to meet a YOS worker once every fortnight for the first six weeks and then once a month to discuss the consequences of offending; and to explore information on jobs and courses.

Reparation was five hours working with 'Groundwork' projects.

In addition, his mother agreed to be supportive throughout his referral order. He subsequently reoffended and has been given a reparation order.

Young Person 2
A 16-year-old boy who received a six-month referral order (and £40 costs) for theft of mail. Victim 2 attended this young person's panel meeting. The youth's father attended his initial panel meeting. His contract required the following activities:

> To address offending behaviour: to meet a YOS worker once every fortnight for the first three months and then once a month for the period of the order to discuss relationships with peers, consequences of reoffending, and [to discuss] employment options with career advisor.

Reparation entailed 19 hours' clearing the local open space with support worker and work at local support centre, training in electrical repairs.

In addition, it was agreed that his father would continue to support him.

Young Person 3
A 16-year-old boy given a four-month referral order and two-month extension both for motoring offences – initially aggravated TWOC. Victims 3 and 4 attended this young person's panel meetings, the first attended his initial panel meeting and the second his extension panel meeting. His mother and brother attended his initial panel meeting. His initial contract required the following:

> To address offending behaviour: to meet a YOS worker to discuss the consequences of offending, peer pressure, alcohol awareness, victim empathy, decision-making, and work on self-esteem.

Reparation took the form of attending the 'Fire Service' reparation programme and completing seven hours with 'Groundwork' projects.

At his extension panel the additional terms of the contract included additional employment and education options and further reparation in the form of 10 hours' direct reparation to the second victim, which involved helping the victim clear tree stumps from his garden (with a sessional supervisor).

Young Person 8
A 13-year-old boy given an eight-month referral order (and £250 costs) for criminal damage. His mother attended all his panel meetings. She was also interviewed (P8). His contract required the following activities:

> To address offending behaviour: to meet support worker once every fortnight for the first four months and monthly thereafter to discuss what will happen if he reoffends, victim awareness, decision making and consequences, and problems at school.

Reparation entailed 20 hours of work with social services to clean access buses.

In addition, it was agreed that his mother and family would support him in completing the order.

Young Person 9
A 12-year-old boy who received a three-month referral order (and £40 costs) for being carried in a stolen car. He did not meet the victim in person, but his mother met with the victim after the initial panel. This meeting was arranged and facilitated by a VLO. The young person's mother was also interviewed (P9). The young person's mother and father both attended the initial panel meeting. The youth's contract required the following activities:

To address offending behaviour: to meet a YOS worker fortnightly for the first half of the order, then monthly thereafter to discuss: victim awareness, peer pressure, and self-esteem.

Reparation was five hours' working with West Yorkshire Fire Service (to be tailored around the young person's needs).

In addition, it was agreed that his parents would fully support him through the order. He has subsequently reoffended and been given a three-month action plan order.

Young Person 10
A 16-year-old boy given a 12-month referral order (and £40 costs) for arson and TWOC. His mother attended his initial panel meeting. His contract required the following activities:

To address offending behaviour: five sessions with Fire Service reparation; Saturday Fire Service session; and to meet support worker once every fortnight and then once a month for the period of the order.

Reparation was to entail 36 hours of work for the victim, if possible to be reviewed at a three-month meeting. In addition, it was agreed as a voluntary activity that he would write a letter of apology to the victim.

Young Person 11
A 17-year-old boy given an eight-month referral order (and £40 costs) for burglary. He attended the initial panel meeting with his mother. His contract required the following activities:

To address offending behaviour: to meet a YOS worker to discuss victim awareness work, consequences of actions, decision making, peer pressure; and work with Connexions regarding training and employment.

Reparation included 29 hours of environmental/charitable work, divided between a model farm (a small local charity providing riding for the disabled) and a voluntary youth club, with support for the sessions in setting up and clearing up.

Preparation for the panel

Most of the young people and parents interviewed said that they felt they had been given enough information about the youth offender panel meeting before attending, albeit they also said that they didn't know what to expect, as the following parent noted:

"Well, I didn't really know what to expect, to be honest, because I'd not really been to anything like that before, so I didn't really know what to expect." (P9)

When asked whether he was properly prepared for the meeting, one young person commented:

"Not really, but I didn't really need to be prepared. I didn't really have nothing to hide. I didn't need to prepare what I was going to say. I just took it as it came really." (YP2)

Some of the young people did not know beforehand that the victim would be attending the meeting. One young person said that the last-minute appearance of the victim had somewhat thrown him, leaving him feeling unprepared (YP3). However, he went on to explain that had he known that the victim was coming he probably would have felt more nervous and might not have turned up.

One young person who was told some days beforehand had the following response when he first found out that the victim might be there: [10]

"They said when I first went that she [the victim] might be going.
How did this make you feel?
Well alright, I just wanted to meet her anyway.
You did want to meet her?
Yes, to say sorry and everything." (YP10)

The panel meeting

All the young people said that the location of the panel meeting was suitable and convenient. Two young people commented on how the YOS had gone out of their way to choose a location that was convenient for them, or at least their parents, to get to. They commented on how informal, 'normal' and 'ordinary' the surroundings of the panel meeting were and how relaxed the panel members tried to make all the participants feel. The experience of the panel meeting was often contrasted starkly to the formality of the courtroom, as another parent noted:

"Well anybody that goes to court can find court a bit daunting, can't they? Especially if they are there for the wrong reasons, such like [her son] was. There was a much more relaxed atmosphere in all the panel meetings. It wasn't anything like a court at all." (P8)

They all said that they were introduced to the other panel members, although there was some uncertainty in some of their minds precisely who the panel members were or what they were supposed to be doing.

---

[10] The interviewer's questions are italicised.

All the young people said that it was made clear to them that if they did not attend the panel meeting or failed to do what was asked of them, they would be returned to court and resentenced. This coercive context was an ever-present feature of the panel meeting, regardless of its informality, as the following young person explained:

> "Did you feel that you had choices as to what would happen to you?
> No, I had no choice at all.
> Did they explain what would happen if you didn't go to the panel?
> Yes. That I could go back to court and get sent to prison." (YP10)

Meeting the victim

Some of the young people felt that they did not have much choice about whether the victim would attend the panel meeting:

> "They asked me, 'what would you think if the woman attended?' You know, the woman that it happened to? And I said that I wouldn't really like it. This was before the panel meeting. Because I just feel weird really. Anyway, she attended anyway, so I didn't have no choice." (YP2)

All but one of the young people who met a victim said that they were nervous before meeting the victim or found the meeting difficult. One young person explained the impact of the meeting:

> "I was shocked that she turned up. I was kind of quiet at first. But when I started talking to her and when she discussed how she felt about it all, I kind of felt a bit better in myself that she actually turned up and came face to face with me." (YP11)

Another young person expressed his mixed feelings about meeting the victim:

> "I wasn't particularly bothered but I was in a way, because I just felt weird. And when I went in, she was, like, emotional. And I apologised to her and I said 'I'm sorry for any inconvenience or any trouble I may have caused you', and I just apologised to her." (YP2)

When asked how he felt when he met the victim, another young person simply replied that he felt "ashamed" (YP8).

One young offender who met one victim at his initial panel meeting and then had a second victim of a later offence (both motoring) attend an extension panel meeting, explained his response to meeting his victims: "I listened to them, but afterwards they started telling me all the problems they had after, I did, like, regret doing it" (YP3).

The mother who, in place of her son, met the victim at a separate meeting after the panel meeting, explained how she felt about this:

> "It was very good actually. I felt I needed to meet with her [the victim] because … well a lot of people initially would think 'well what were the parents like?' You know. And I wanted to give a bit of background about us … there was a lot mixed up with it so I didn't want her [the victim] immediately passing judgement and just thinking that he were a real bad 'un and his parents just didn't give a damn. So I felt it necessary to meet with her and explain this. We spoke about each other's backgrounds and what difference it had made to her and I think when I came out of there, I think she really felt quite sorry for me to be honest … I'm glad I met her, she's a really nice lady. We got on very well and I think she saw a different view on the whole situation. And I made it plain that I didn't condone him … I was quite horrified when she told me just what damage had been done and how it affected her and her family. But I enjoyed the meeting. I felt it necessary." (P9)

All the young people said that they listened to what the victim had to say, and this often had a significant impact upon the offender. One young person's response, when asked how he felt having heard what the victim had to say, was typical of others: "Bad for what I had done" (YP10).

All the young people were asked if they thought it right that the victim should be invited to attend panel meetings. This elicited a mixed response. Only one young person said 'no' to the question, and he was the only young person who did not actually meet his victim. When asked why, he gave the following explanation: "Because nobody really wants to meet them [their victims]" (YP9).

One of the young people who said he thought it was right that victims should be invited to attend, when asked to explain why, answered as follows: "Because it helped me, it could help other people" (YP3). A third young person, asked the same question, expressed a certain degree of ambiguity that reflected others' sentiments:

> "Oooh. I don't know. Not really. If the person [offender] wants the person [victim] to be there then fair enough. But obviously, we are in the wrong and the victim really should have a right to be there anyway, shouldn't they?" (YP2)

Having a say

All except one of the young people said that they had been given a full opportunity to have their say and to explain themselves during the meeting.

> "Were there things that you would have liked to have said but didn't?
> Yes.
> Like what things?
> Just that I didn't mean to do it and stuff like that.
> Why didn't you feel that you had an opportunity to do that?
> Because she was speaking and she looked at me as if she wasn't listening. So, I just thought, well I'm not going to say nowt." (YP10)

The younger offenders were understandably more overawed by the occasion and less likely to feel comfortable in a room full of adults. The parent of a 13-year-old commented:

> "He certainly had a chance to have his say. We all did. We were all given a chance to speak. Everybody was that was there." (P8)

All of the young people were accompanied to the initial panel meeting by at least one parent (usually, but not exclusively, the mother) and felt that they were there to help and support them. For some, the presence of a parent was embarrassing. One young person, when asked how he felt with his parents being at the meeting, explained: "Well, I didn't like it, to be honest, because they listened to the victim" (YP3). Both parents echoed this sentiment. One commented that she felt it was:

> "Pretty embarrassing really. I suppose you could say it's not something that most parents want to be going through at all." (P8)

However, the parents did not feel that the panel members either were judgemental or made them feel particularly awkward.

Procedural justice

All the young people said that they understood what was going on during the panel meeting, they were treated with respect by the panel members, and the panel process was fair. This high level of procedural satisfaction reflects the survey findings and is in line with findings from other restorative justice initiatives around the world (Strang et al, 1999; Daly, 2001). This is significant in that, as Tyler (1990) suggests, people are more likely to comply with a regulatory order that they perceive to be procedurally just. There is some evidence emerging from the RISE research into the community conferencing initiative in Canberra that citizens' personal judgement that the law is moral may depend upon their judgement that the human agents of the legal system have treated them with respect (Sherman et al, 2003). The more legitimacy that such agents (namely conference facilitators and panel members) can create, the more likely they are to impact positively upon higher levels of future compliance with the law and reduce reoffending.

Except for one young person (see above) all the young people said that the victim had listened to them and treated them with respect. For at least one young person, although he felt that he was treated fairly and with due respect during the panel meeting and the referral order process, he did not feel that the referral order itself was a proportionate or fair response to what he had done (in his case, criminal damage). Thus the *internal* legitimacy of the process was circumscribed by the lack of *external* legitimacy of the criminal justice response to his actions. For him, the referral order was: "Not fair really, because it were for nowt, for something stupid" (YP1). The following exchange clarifies the young person's ambiguous thinking:

> *"Did you feel you were listened to by the panel members?*
> Oh yes, they listened to me.
> *What about the victim? Did you feel you were listened to by the victim?*
> Yes, when I was talking he was listening and that.
> *Did he respond to what you had to say?*
> I didn't really say much to him, because I didn't really want to. Because he got me arrested and that, you know. So, I didn't want to talk to him.
> *Did you feel that you were treated with respect by the panel members?*
> Yes.
> *Did you feel that you were treated with respect by the victim?*
> Yes. He did. But I didn't treat him with respect. He was all friendly and all that.
> *Why did you not treat him with respect?*
> Because he got me arrested. So why should I?" (YP1)

No matter how fair or procedurally just the panel meeting may be, it will be tainted by wider perceptions of legitimacy and justice.

Purpose of the panel meeting

When asked what they thought the main purpose of the panel meeting was, the following responses were given:

- "Just clear up what I had to do."
- "To explain what I had done.'
- "To, just really just to see what I had to do and for the victim to tell me, to let me know, how she felt."
- "It was to find out what I was like and to see how I was coping with things."
- "Trying to tell you not to get into trouble and that."
- "Basically to find out what I had done and to find out how I feel and if I'd realised that it was wrong."
- "To try and turn myself around."

When asked, most felt that one of the purposes was to help them. None of them thought that the panel was there specifically to punish them. One young person when asked if one of the purposes of the panel was to punish answered:

> "No, I wouldn't say that, no. I were just, the only way I'd say it was like a punishment in a way was because I didn't know that the woman was going to turn up until I got there." (YP2)

One young person had the following to say when asked whether a purpose of the panel was to punish or to help him:

> "To help, I think. The whole thing is to help.
> *So did you feel that you were being punished at all?*
> No. Not really. Well, yes the things I had to do, and that, but the other stuff is trying to help me in a way." (YP10)

Apology

At panel meetings an apology can be a powerful emotional experience for both victim and young person, where honestly given and accepted. A majority of the young people derived significant personal benefit and satisfaction from apologising directly to the victim, as the following discussion reflects:

> "I felt nervous to speak to her, but after I did speak to her, she was a nice woman and I could see that she were like emotional. So I just made a point to just apologise to her properly. And not just said 'Oh, I'm sorry', like that, I didn't say just like 'Uh, I'm sorry', like I didn't mean it. And I said it like I did mean it and did say 'I'm very sorry' ...
> *Did you feel that she accepted that apology?*
> Yes.
> *What made you feel that, did she do anything or say anything in particular that made you feel she had accepted the apology?*
> She was just emotional. And she held my hand and she goes 'thanks for that'. And then I just knew." (YP2)

For some of the young people apologising was the primary purpose of the victim's presence:

> "What happened was that they asked me if I wanted him to come. And I said ... well they asked me if it would be alright if he came. And I said 'yes'. If you say 'no' then they won't let him come.
> *So, why did you say 'yes'?*
> So that I could say 'sorry' to him.
> *Did you say 'sorry' to him?*
> Yes.

How did that make you feel?
A bit better.
Do you think that he felt better when you said 'sorry' to him?
Well, it might have done a little bit but he was still angry." (YP8)

The one young person who did not meet his victim directly, nevertheless did write a letter of apology to the victim. This also had benefits for him:

"*How did that [writing a letter of apology] make you feel?*
Better.
Why did you feel better?
Because she wasn't angry any more." (YP9)

The mother of one of the young boys commented:

"But it was a good thing for him to meet his victim and the victim to meet him. I think it was good on both cases. Because, you know, it just helped [her son] realise the situation that if you do something to somebody, there are chances that you will meet them again and you have to apologise. I think it was probably one of the best things to do, to meet your victim. It always is better I think. And it gave [her son] a chance to give a proper apology and he did write a letter to him [the victim]." (P8)

One young person who subsequently met his victim sometime after the panel meeting which the victim had attended, commented on the experience:

"It was kind of shocking, really, that she stood and talked to me. But it was nice, it was good to have a chat with her. I mean my mate, who was involved in it [the burglary] as well. He knows her daughter, so we started talking to her as well. And that was strange. But after meeting the victim again after the referral order it was okay." (YP11)

However, for one young person the apology was clearly not offered voluntarily:

"*Did you apologise to the victim?*
I had to …
Why do you say that you had to?
Because they said: 'Are you going to say sorry?', and then I said: 'No, I don't want to'. And they said: 'Well, you're going to have to'. So, I said: 'sorry'.
How did that make you feel?
Nowt really." (YP1)

This suggests that, for offenders as well as victims, coerced or forced apologies may be of little or no value. To be meaningful, for both parties, apologies should be sincere and spontaneous.

Where letters of apology are sent it may also be useful to provide feedback to young people about what is done with them or any response from victims, as implied by one offender when asked how useful he thought writing the letter of apology to the victim had been:

> "I don't know, I don't know what she's done with it. She could have just thrown it away or owt." (YP10)

Some young people were uncertain whether their letter had actually been sent to the victim. What to do with letters of apology and whether these are passed on to victims were concerns also raised by panel members and RJ Team staff in interviews.

Devising the contract

There were mixed feelings about how much input the young people and their parents felt that they were able to exert. Some felt that the requirements were imposed upon them, while others felt that they had some significant input into, and control over, the agreed outcomes. One young person felt he had some considerable say in the devising of the contract:

> *"Did you contribute to the discussion about which activities you were going to do in the contract?*
> Oh it were all put together, really, it was a bunch of ideas and they were all put into one and then we all realised which would be the easiest to do.
> *But did you feel that you had a contribution to that?*
> Oh yes.
> *You didn't feel …*
> Pushed into it? No." (YP11)

For this young person, the fact that he had contributed to the contract gave him an incentive to ensure that he complied with its terms as he subsequently explained:

> "I'm glad I actually discussed with them what I was going to do rather than them saying 'this is what you're doing'. It were a lot easier. If they had said: 'this is what you are doing', I would have felt a bit down about myself, but you could do in either situation, I did commit a very serious offence." (YP11)

Others had a less positive experience:

> *"Did you contribute to the ideas about what should be in the contract?*
> No, not really.

Who suggested them?
Well, I suggested the letter of apology, but all the other ones were by [the YOS worker].
Did you agree because you felt you had to agree or because you thought they were appropriate?
No, because I had to." (YP10)

Parents likewise experienced slightly different degrees of control over and input into contractual deliberations:

"We didn't know what he would be doing until later on, they gave him some suggestions what it could have been. And we said, 'Oh yeah, that sounds fair enough'. But we knew that they wouldn't give him anything too silly or too daft for him. I mean cleaning buses... actually he quite likes buses and stuff. So it was something ... they asked him what hobbies and things he had, and they sort of connected both things together, for him to do his like community service thing, as we called it, so that he was actually given something he actually enjoyed doing. Even though it was a chore of cleaning buses, he actually enjoyed it." (P8)

The experience of the other parent was rather different:

"I think they [the panel] basically decided what the plan was. I didn't really have any say-so. It was sort of decided what he was going to do. He was okay about that ... It was more or less presented, there wasn't really any choice. Because of the nature of the crime they had decided what it would be and that was it really." (P9)

Most interviewees felt that the details of the contracts were, by and large, fair and appropriate.

Views on victims

Young people were asked how they felt about the victim after the meeting. For some there appears to have been a shift in attitudes and acknowledgement of the harm caused. For example, one young person commented: "I feel sorry for her really, the damage that we caused and the stuff that we took. It must be really upsetting." (YP11)

Young people were also asked how they thought the victim felt after the meeting.

"I think that she was relieved in a way. Because then she knew, because when we were doing what we were doing we didn't really think, because it was just stupid. And she would have felt really relieved, in a way, instead of looking out her window all the time." (YP2)

One young person, when asked if they thought that they had been able to help make up for the harm caused to the victim by their actions, gave the following response:

> "Not to her really. I doubt she would feel so but that's not my fault. We offered, well I offered to do some work for her, but she didn't want me to, so." (YP10)

This suggests that for many, making amends was not necessarily a feasible aim of panel meetings.

Nevertheless, most of the young people left the panel meeting feeling better for it and the encounter with their victim, in particular. When asked how he felt at the end of the meeting, one young person commented as follows: "I felt proud of myself in a way, for apologising to the woman and facing it up" (YP2).

Compliance and review meetings

Young people said that they were given sufficient support and assistance by the YOS in completing the terms of their contract. One young person who had found the nature of the community reparation to be particularly unrewarding had been able to change what he did and was appreciative of this flexibility.

A number of young people who had felt that they had had some significant contribution to the discussions about the appropriate terms in the contract said that this had given them an incentive to complete the contract in full.: "It gave me more of a reason to do them [the activities]", as one offender explained (YP2). However, they were all aware that failure to complete the contract may result in them being referred back to court, as the following young person explained when asked what his main motivation for completing the contract had been: "Because if I didn't do them then I would go back to court and get re-sentenced so I might as well get it over and done with" (YP1).

Most found the review meetings useful, if somewhat brief in duration. Those young people who had significant numbers of the same panel members attend review meetings found this valuable. Where there had not been continuity of membership, young people commented adversely about this.

Most of the young people felt good about themselves for having successfully completed the contract. All the young people said that at the end of the referral order they felt able to put the offence behind them and move on with their lives. One young person described his feelings once he had completed the referral order, as follows: "Pleased I could get back on track" (YP3).

Keeping out of trouble

Most of the young people were clear that the experience of the referral order had helped keep them out of trouble, as illustrated by the following comments: "It's helped me keep off the streets and stop getting into trouble, yes" (YP10). Another young person, when asked whether his attitudes toward his offence had changed in the light of his experiences, responded:

> "Yes, yes it has.
> *In what way?*
> I've stopped nicking cars. I can't even touch them. I've stopped doing all of that."
> (YP3)

Asked the same question, the following young person also suggested that the referral order experience had impacted upon his views:

> "Yes.
> *In what way?*
> Just not to do stupid things, and get into trouble. Not to do stupid things really.
> *Was there anything particular about the referral order that made you feel that way?*
> Not really. Oh yes. Cleaning the streets, that were just bad because one time my mates came up with me and they were all taking the mick out of me. And I just thought, 'never again'. I don't want to be doing this again. So it just made me realise." (YP2)

However, two of the seven young people were subsequently reconvicted for new offences, although the mother of one of them was categorical that the referral order had helped ensure that her son had not got involved in the same offence for which he had received the original order:

> "I think seeing some of the things that can happen when people are driving stolen cars. I mean he certainly hasn't got into a stolen car again, nothing like that. I think that did hit home … I suppose their main role is to try and ensure that it doesn't happen again and with regards that type of offence then, yes it has worked." (P9)

The young person himself was the only one interviewed who did not feel that the referral order had helped keep him out of trouble. Moreover, he was the only young person not to meet his victim directly, albeit he did not attribute a causal link. He explained that: "It's just that I didn't change my friends who I got into trouble with" (YP9). His mother felt that, if anything, the referral order had been insufficiently intensive and had not provided enough support for her son to address his underlying problems, which she attributed to his anger in relation to the death of his elder sister a couple of years earlier.

"So it probably wasn't as severe or involved as it should have been ... The aim of it is to get them on the right track and to keep them from the same kind of offence, which, that has worked. But it has not worked in terms of not getting into any more trouble if you like... Like, [the YOS worker] brought this form for him to fill in about different feelings, what did he think about this, that and the other? And then he [the YOS worker] just picked it up, next time he came. There was no real discussion. I think it would have been better if he had worked with him on that at the same time. I mean you have a meeting and they come and basically it's the same thing being said each time. I mean obviously I want the support to help [her son]." (P9)

All the other young people said that the referral order had helped keep them out of trouble, albeit sometimes for different reasons. When asked if the referral order had helped to keep him out of trouble, one said:

"Oh yes. Definitely, I've just realised how lucky I was to get a referral order rather than been sentenced or getting a really big fine or what have you.
What about your attitudes towards your offence and offending, have they changed as a consequence of the referral order?
Oh yes, I stay out of the way of trouble now. Not a chance." (YP11)

Another young person explained that the decision to keep out of trouble was one he had taken by himself, but that this decision was reinforced and supported by the referral order experience (YP10). For this young person, the value of the referral order was ultimately recognised, although reluctantly.

Views on the youth justice system

Young people were asked, as a result of their experience of the referral order, whether their views about the youth justice system had changed.

"Well, before my referral order I didn't really think about it, if you know what I mean, but after it's good how they do it. It's ... The way they are, the way they treat you, it couldn't be any better really, they really are nice people." (YP11)

All interviewees were asked if, on the basis of their experience, the service provided by the YOS could be improved, and if so how. One young person remarked: "No, not at all. It were ... Actually, really, really surprisingly, it were good, it were good" (YP11).

The only person who identified specific improvements was the mother who, cited earlier, felt that the limited intervention triggered by the referral order had failed to address her son's needs:

"Well I think the meetings should be more than once a fortnight. I know it's difficult because they must have a lot of kids to deal with. But I certainly think it should be more than once a fortnight … I think there should be more involvement on that side of things where they are doing a bit more. Apart from that I don't really know what else they can do. I mean it's only a short-term, three months, it's not very long." (P9)

6

Contracts and compliance

Youth offender contracts

A sample of 302 contracts where the first panel meeting was held in 2004 were analysed for the purpose of this research. These contracts were analysed by case and therefore incorporate extensions (see later). They exclude panel meetings that were held for young people who failed to attend or who were subsequently referred back to court. It also excludes two contracts signed in other YOS areas and subsequently transferred to the Leeds service.

The length of the initial orders that reached a successful contract is set out in Figure 14. It shows that nearly half (47%) were for 3 months, and some 86% were for 6 months or less.

Just under a fifth (18%) of panel meetings that produced an agreed contract in the sample subsequently resulted in an extension to the referral order length (n=56). Figure 15 provides an overview of the length of extensions given.

Figure 14: Length of initial referral order that reached a successful contract (%)

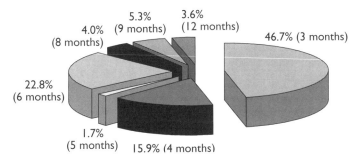

Figure 15: Length of extensions to referral orders that reached a contract (%)

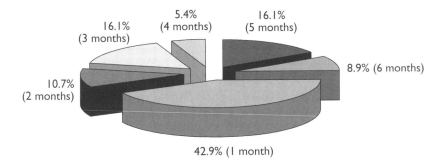

Figure 16: Length including extensions of referral order that reached a sucessful contract (%)

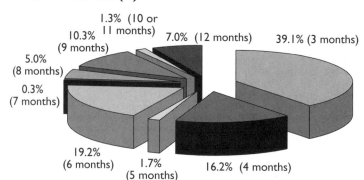

The average length of a referral order (including extensions) received by young people in the sample was 5.4 months (Figure 16).

According to the contract data, some 59 young people in 2004 did not attend at least one of the initial or extension panel meetings arranged for them.[11] However, 34 of these (some 58%) did go on to have a successful panel meeting at which a contract was agreed. According to the records, approximately a third of those who did not attend for an initial panel meeting had reoffended before being sent back to court.

Contractual conditions

Each youth offender contract comprised four elements:

(1) compulsory activities aimed at addressing the young person's offending behaviour and to help him or her not to commit further offences;
(2) compulsory reparation activities;
(3) voluntary activities;
(4) ways in which the parent or carer will support the young person to complete the contract.

Compulsory activities

Compulsory activities generally entailed young people meeting with their YOS worker or attending specific sessions. Meetings with YOS workers were primarily identified for the purposes of discussing a specific combination of subjects drawing upon the following:

---

[11] This excludes review, final or emergency panel meetings.

- victim awareness and victim empathy;
- consequences of offending/effects of actions;
- anti-social behaviour;
- peer pressure;
- school attendance;
- anger management;
- decision making;
- drugs and alcohol awareness;
- health and smoking;
- lifestyle;
- self-esteem;
- careers and employment; and
- race awareness.

An analysis of the youth offender contracts shows that victim awareness is a regular element in addressing young people's offending behaviour.

Contractual requirements were largely couched in terms of the regularity of the meetings with YOS workers. Figure 17 shows that in more than three quarters (78%) of contracts one of two standard approaches was used. Meetings were to be held either once a fortnight then once a month (the latter usually for the second half of the referral order term), or as and when required as determined by the YOS worker. This latter approach clearly left greater discretion in the hands of the workers to adapt the regularity of meeting to the perceived needs of the young person.

There were a limited number of programmes, initiatives or sessions that were specifically identified in the contracts. Considerable use was made of two particular groupwork-based schemes that combined an element of reparation with activities to address the young person's offending behaviour. These were a Fire Service Reparation project targeted at young people involved in vehicle crime and/or arson, and a Saturday Group, run fortnightly for young people not in need of

Figure 17: Regularity of meetings with YOS workers to discuss activities as set down in the initial contract (%)

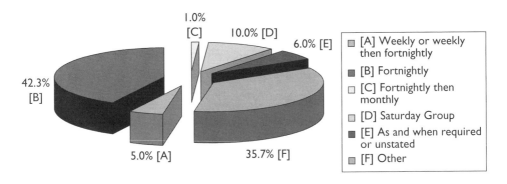

individual support but who might benefit from groupwork focused on issues of re-offending. There would seem to be scope to develop a wider portfolio of specialist programmes and activities from which panels might draw.

Reparation activities

All contracts included some kind of designated reparation activity. The most common form of reparation was 'community reparation'. There was very little direct reparation to victims. A letter of apology was a compulsory element of reparation in 9% of cases and was included as a voluntary element with a further 3% of contracts. A letter of apology was a significantly more common outcome where there had been some identifiable form of victim involvement. Some three-fifths of contracts involving a letter of apology as a compulsory element appeared to have some form of victim involvement. According to the contracts, a victim attended in 4%, and there was victim involvement in a further 16% of cases. This wider victim involvement frequently took the form of the presence at the panel meeting of one of the VLOs, presumably to present the victim's perspective.

Moreover, a letter of apology was much more likely in relation to referral orders initially made for 12 months. Here, the figures rise to 36% for a letter of apology as a compulsory element and 18% as a voluntary element of the contract ($n=11$). Apart from this, any other form of direct reparation was only mentioned (sometimes only as a possibility) in less than 2% of contracts. This is considerably lower than the direct reparation and letters of apology found in the evaluation of the referral order pilots (Newburn et al, 2002, p 29).

Community reparation took a wide variety of forms, requiring young people to work a certain number of hours in diverse environments and for different purposes. Some of these activities contribute to local initiatives and community improvement in innovative ways, and draw young people into constructive activities.

However, it was often unclear how the reparation activity related to the offending behaviour itself and that it was more likely to be conditioned by the availability of specific schemes of community reparation, combined with the young person's interests and preferences. One interesting departure from this was the production of posters about the young person's offending behaviour which could be used for the purpose of prevention programmes. The lack of correspondence between reparation and the offence committed (outside of those examples mentioned about) may reflect the fact that victims appeared only to have a limited input into proposals, for or ideas about, suitable reparation. Consideration might be given to strengthening this element of reparation programmes.

Figure 18: Range of contractual hours of reparation (%)

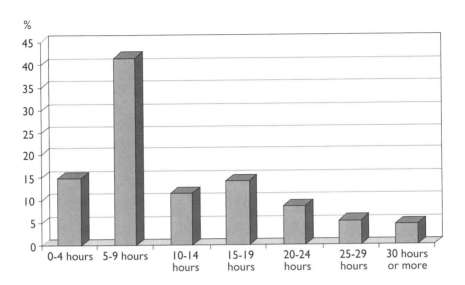

Generally, reparation appears to have been considered primarily in terms of the number of hours required. Figure 18 outlines the range of numbers of hours of reparation given across all the contracts (where the information was available).

Figure 19 shows that the number of hours of reparation broadly corresponds to the length of the referral order. The vast majority (95%) of three- or four-month orders (including extension) involved less than 10 hours' and 84% of five- to seven-month orders included between 10 and 19 hours' reparation. The majority of eight- and nine-month orders (63%) included reparation of between 20 and 29 hours. Half of referral orders for 10–12 months involved reparation activities of 30 hours

Figure 19: Hours of reparation by length of order (including extensions) (%)

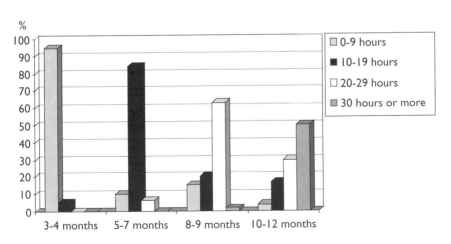

or more. As such, the overall quantity of reparation hours is broadly in line with national guidance.

There was some concern about the lack of clarity over distinctions between activities aimed at reducing the young person's offending behaviour and reparation. In a limited number of contracts, specified activities conflated elements designed to address the young person's offending behaviour with reparation activities. For example, attendance at the 'Saturday Group' and 'Fire Service crime course' constituted elements of reparation and crime prevention. These activities were collectively identified in nearly 9% of contracts. In this instance, distinctions between reparative activities and activities aimed at addressing the young person's offending behaviour are neither self-evident nor clear for all concerned. This can send confused messages both to victims and offenders about the value and role of reparation within referral orders. Other unusual forms of reparation included 'work with an appropriate agency to discuss bereavement' and 'helping around the house'.

Voluntary activities

Voluntary activities were included in more than half (55%) of all youth offender contracts. As already mentioned, writing a letter of apology was often included as a voluntary, rather than a compulsory, element of a youth offender contract. This was more likely to be the case where the victim had not yet been approached or asked whether they were willing to consent to receive a letter of apology. As a consequence, it was not known, at the time of writing the contract, whether the letter would be sent to the victim. Where a victim had consented to an apology and this had been agreed by the victim, it was more likely to be a compulsory element of the contract.

Other voluntary activities often related to: [12]

- work around the home/domestic chores (16%);
- improving relations with parents/coming home at certain times/informing parents of whereabouts (9%);
- school/college attendance or homework (10%);
- attendance at sports activities (10%);
- actively looking for work/apprenticeships or attendance at employment-based courses (such as HYPE, Connexions) (11%);
- attendance at other classes, including Positive Activities for Young People (PAYP) (13%);
- keeping away from certain peers (2%);

---

[12] These figures relate to the percentage of those contracts that identified a voluntary activity (n=166).

- staying away from certain locations (2%);
- apology to victim (5%);
- payments to parents to cover court-ordered costs/compensation (6%); and
- additional voluntary work or reparation (6%).

Support from parents/carers

This element of the contract usually entailed identifying, by name, the parent(s) or family members, usually those attending the meeting, who agreed to support the young person, usually in non-specified ways. This voluntary element of the contract was completed in 78% of cases. In a further 1% of cases it was used to identify the fact that a parent had not attended the panel meeting.

Compliance

Table 9 shows the recorded outcomes for referral orders within our research period. The figure of 69% of young people successfully completing their contracts is in line with, but slightly lower than, the figure of 74% from the national pilots (Newburn et al, 2002). It should be noted that 52 of the orders had not yet been given a recorded outcome in the YOS database, normally because they had not yet finished, or the final review had not yet been held.

Table 10 provides a breakdown of the recorded outcomes by gender. There is a broad similarity between boys and girls, although a slightly higher proportion of boys successfully completed their referral orders.

Table 9: Referral orders with recorded outcomes, April to September 2004

Outcome	Number	% of total
Successfully completed	112	68.7
Partially completed (YP reoffended)	25	15.3
Partially completed (missed sessions)	9	5.5
Breached substitute community penalty – not completed/terminated	6	3.7
Referred elsewhere or substitute other programme – not completed	5	3.1
Breached (other)	5	3.1
No information	1	0.6
Total	163	100

Note: No outcome has yet been recorded for 52 referral orders

Table 10: Referral orders with recorded outcomes, April to September 2004 by gender

Outcome	Female		Male	
	Number	%	Number	%
Successfully completed	26	63.4	86	70.5
Partially completed (YP reoffended)	1	2.4	4	3.3
Partially completed (missed sessions)	9	22.0	16	13.1
Breached substitute community penalty – not completed/ terminated	5	12.2	4	3.3
Referred elsewhere or substitute other programme – not completed	0	0.0	6	4.9
Breached (other)	0	0.0	5	4.1
No information	0	0.0	1	0.8
Total	41	100	122	100

Note: No outcome has yet been recorded for 14 referral orders

Reoffending rates

The timescale for this research did not allow for the analysis of meaningful reoffending rates in relation to our research cohort. However, research into one year reconviction[13] rates from the national 2003 cohort (Home Office, 2005, p 8) shows that referral orders compare favourably with all other court disposals. The 12-month reconviction rate among the 5,895 young people given a referral order in 2003 was 37.1%, significantly lower than the rates for other first-tier penalties, including a discharge (51.9%), a fine (57.7%) and a reparation order (62.3%), and considerably lower than rates for community penalties (average 67.7%) and custody (69.4%). The 2003 cohort also showed statistically significant reductions as compared to previous years for offenders given a referral order (down 6.5% on the 2002 cohort).

Inevitably, variations in reconviction rates across different disposals are largely explained by differences in the characteristics of the young offenders given each disposal. Those young offenders given a referral order, on first appearance in court, are likely to have lower intrinsic risk of offending as compared to those given a

---

[13] Reconviction, here, is defined as all reoffending that ends with either a conviction at court or a formal pre-court disposal.

custodial sentence, for example. Consequently, reconviction rates for pre-court disposals are even lower than for a court-ordered disposal such as a referral order. According to the 2003 cohort, reconviction for final warnings and reprimands stood at 19.7%.

In interview, YOS staff endorsed this optimistic view, suggesting that referral orders are impacting more than other interventions on reoffending. However, it was also recognised that many of the young people given referral orders were more likely not to reoffend in any case, as one senior member of staff noted:

> "… we're getting young people on the first rung of the ladder of their criminal career and for a lot of these young people who do offend, who get referral orders, it is often just a blip and they're not habitual offenders …"

Nevertheless, some panel members felt they were able to identify positive changes brought about in young people:

> "It's very rewarding to turn a kid around, you can see them very aggressive, sometimes you'll click on something, they open up and you'll get somewhere."

7

Conclusions

Integrating victims in restorative youth justice

Referral orders and youth offender panels remain in their infancy. Traditionally, the core tasks of youth justice agencies have been defined in terms of processing young offenders. Consequently, work with victims both is novel and sometimes sits awkwardly alongside practitioners' other demands. It is often difficult for youth justice agencies to devote time and personnel to work relating to victims. Yet the integration of victims is central both to a restorative justice philosophy and to delivering a youth justice system with integrity.

Recent, 'impressionistic' research by JUSTICE reinforced the pilot research findings that the national implementation of referral orders remains uneven and variable. The report commented on the evolving nature of practice across the country within a "fast-changing environment" (Tickell and Akester, 2004, p 84). Some Youth Offender Services (YOSs) rely upon subcontracting victim work to dedicated mediation and reparation specialist organisations, others (like the Leeds YOS) employ in-house victim liaison officers (VLOs), and still others disperse victim work among referral order staff. In theory, the latter approach has the most transformative long-term potential, lying in the ideal of all YOS staff as the guardians of a victim perspective and restorative justice champions. However, in the context of an evolving service with competing demands and against reluctant cultural barriers, the advantages of a service provided by dedicated, appropriately trained and skilled staff sensitive to the needs and experiences of victims of crime are significant, as this research testifies. The success of the Leeds initiative has resulted in all five YOSs across West Yorkshire employing dedicated VLOs.

The national picture reinforces our research findings that the take-up rate of victims attending panel meetings is comparatively low. Hence, involving victims in a meaningful and sensitive way within the youth offender panel process constitutes one of the greatest challenges for YOS staff in realising the full potential of referral orders. While it is important for the young person that initial panel meetings should be held as soon as possible after the offence and court appearance, national standards requiring the initial panel meeting to be held within 20 working days of the referral order being issued by the court often militate against high levels of victim involvement at initial panel meetings. However, the challenges presented by such time constraints should not serve as easy justifications for low levels of victim attendance at panel meetings. Moreover, there are ways of encouraging face-to-face meetings between young people and their victims subsequent to an initial panel meeting as a part of the young offender's reparation activities.

Overly simplistic targets for victim attendance may ignore two important insights from this research: first, victims (as well as young offenders and their families) can significantly benefit from contact and liaison with the YOS and input into the referral order process, short of attending a panel meeting; and, second, the need to acknowledge that there are limitations to victim involvement. Some victims, for very good reasons, will not want to meet their offender and would prefer to leave the process of punishing and reintegrating the offender to professionals. There may be limits on both victims' capacities to see offenders in a positive light and offenders' willingness to repair the harm caused or to empathise with the victim. Notable among the reasons for victims' negative judgements of offenders were the offender not showing remorse and not taking responsibility for what he or she had done. Likewise, from the perspective of the victim, there are limits to the feasibility of restoration, as many young people who have offended will not necessarily be able to make sufficient reparation. Nevertheless, it is also clear from this study that, where sensitively treated, victims have much to benefit from restorative approaches to justice, particularly at an emotional level. Effective victim engagement in the context of referral orders enables victims to be treated more humanely and with due respect to their interests and needs than is otherwise normally the case within criminal justice interventions.

Good-quality victim liaison work is both time-consuming and labour-intensive. The employment of dedicated VLOs affords a way of ensuring that victims' needs and interests are given due significance within the youth offender panel process and the course of the referral order. Furthermore, specialist VLOs can, and do, act as champions of the victims' perspective within the YOS as a whole and ensure that victims are accorded the appropriate role and voice that they deserve, and that the original legislation intended. However, one unintended consequence of providing dedicated VLOs can be that they may deflect responsibility from other YOS staff and, hence, may do less to transform the culture and workings of the organisation as a whole.

Victims who had contact with the RJ Team accorded to it very high levels of satisfaction. Nevertheless, the work of the RJ Team, which began in 2004, remains in its early stages of development. While important first steps have been taken in integrating a victim perspective into the centre of service delivery, more work remains to be done to increase victim involvement and raise victim awareness both within the referral order process and the work of the YOS more generally.

The experiences presented in this research also point to the need to clarify, for all concerned, distinctions between work that is aimed to address young people's offending behaviour and prevent future offending, on the one hand, and reparation work, on the other hand. This would benefit both victims and young people involved, so that they are clear on the nature and form of reparation. In so doing, it would send clearer messages about the value and role of particular activities, notably the centrality of reparation within restorative justice.

Involving community volunteers

Despite these obvious limitations, this research suggests that youth offender panels provide a positive forum in which to address the consequences of young people's offending behaviour in novel and different ways. In this, the involvement of community panel members has been a central element of the changes. Although not unproblematic, it may nevertheless be an important safeguard against the excesses of managerialist pressures on youth justice with their emphasis on speeding up processes, efficiency benefits and performance measurement (Crawford and Newburn, 2002). These administrative requirements can serve to undermine the normative appeal of restorative justice-inspired interventions. Ensuring diverse volunteer involvement in panels can lead to the inclusion of a broader range of approaches and values. It may also lead to the development of localised practices that, because they are fostered, determined and owned by volunteers, are relatively resistant to the demands of bureaucratic managerialism. The participation of ordinary citizens in the deliberative processes of youth justice can help ensure that proceedings that may otherwise be dominated by technical, bureaucratic or managerial demands also accord with the emotional and expressive needs of those involved in responses to crime, notably victims. It can facilitate the 'opening up' of otherwise introspective professional values, whereby practitioners are guided by detached and disinterested performance standards, often of a kind which are more concerned with internal organisational priorities than responsiveness to public interests. The experience of the youth offender panels in this research is testimony to the seriousness and thoughtfulness that lay people can bring to such forums and to the task of facilitating discussion.

The involvement of volunteers can help make use of a range of locally-based interventions and opportunities for reparation. It may also help to encourage greater synergy between formal and informal systems of control. In so doing, it can promote the importance of local capacity and local knowledge, and contribute, in small part, to restoring the deliberative control of justice to citizens. As such, the experience of youth offender panels has much to contribute to and learn from debates about 'community justice' that have been stimulated by the recent experiment to establish a Community Justice Centre in north Liverpool.

Nevertheless, working with volunteers as equal partners in an inclusive process presents real challenges to the way in which professional YOS staff work. There is clearly still more that can be done in relation to the involvement of volunteers as a broader resource in delivering a form of justice that links panels to the wider communities in which they are located. Crucially, however, the involvement of community representatives should not serve to operate at the expense of direct victim input. While community volunteers may feel capable of bringing a victim perspective through their own role, as an indirect or secondary victim of the crime, this should not be used as a surrogate for victim attendance and input.

Furthermore, volunteer involvement raises questions regarding their representativeness. If lay involvement is intended to reflect the parties' 'peers' or the general citizenry, then this accords a significant import to their representative composition. Inversely, lay involvement may also affront cherished notions of 'non-partisanship' that are key criteria in the legitimate exercise of power, particularly in criminal justice, both at a normative level and in terms of how justice is experienced by individuals. There is an ambiguity in that the more attached to the community lay panel members are, the less likely they are to hold the required 'detached stance' that constitutes a central value in establishing facilitator neutrality and legitimacy. The more that facilitators or panel members represent particular interests or value systems the greater the danger that the interests of one of the principal parties may become sidelined or lost altogether.

Ironically, it is exactly this pressure to provide neutral and detached facilitators that increases the likelihood of the professionalisation of lay panel members and the formalisation of otherwise fluid and open restorative processes. Experience suggests that, over time, schemes come to rely upon a group of 'core' volunteers, who increasingly are seen as semi-professionals by virtue of their work turnover, their training and experience. As a result, panel members may begin to look and behave more like 'quasi-professionals' than ordinary lay people. In this context, lay volunteers raise questions about the appropriate competencies and skills that particular personnel should have in delivering a given service, and hence, about the nature and quality of the service to be delivered, as well as the accountability of volunteers and panel meeting outcomes.

Recent MORI research for the Home Office shows that not only do the British public know very little about youth offending services, but also they are not typically rated as being particularly effective (Page et al, 2004). Confidence and familiarity are interconnected. Considerably more could be done at both the local and national levels to address the lack of public knowledge and understanding about the restorative justice processes employed in youth justice and, more specifically, the operation of youth offender panels. As Hough and Roberts recognise, "there is a pressing need to improve the quality of information available to the public about crime and justice – and this obviously includes youth crime and youth justice" (2004, p 46). Raising the public profile of referral orders, the role of volunteers and victims therein, and the benefits of direct and community reparation schemes, might both enhance the recruitment of additional numbers of volunteers serving as community panel members and foster greater public confidence.

The future of referral orders

This research has shown that panels provide a constructive and participatory forum in which to address young people's offending behaviour and to deliberate upon reparation to the victim and/or community. Their informal atmosphere and inclusive practice allow young people, their parents or carers, victims (where they attend), community panel members and YOS staff, opportunities to discuss the nature and consequences of a young person's offending, as well as how to respond to this in ways that seek to repair the harm done and to attempt to address the causes of the young person's offending behaviour.

However, there remain legitimate concerns about the use of referral orders in cases of trivial or less serious offending, where the level of intervention required by a referral order (at least three months in duration) may appear out of proportion to the behaviour that triggered it. While the amendments to referral orders have helped lessen this difficulty – by making the order discretionary for non-imprisonable offences – they have not removed it, as some minor offences are imprisonable. There is some evidence that the referral order has replaced a conditional discharge in a number of cases, thus heralding a significantly greater interventionism and 'tariff increase'.

In addition, there is genuine unease about the possible 'net-widening' and 'mesh-thinning' effects of such orders (Cohen, 1985), as young people are potentially drawn into and through the youth justice system more rapidly and the intensiveness of interventions may increase. This is particularly evident where young people have not previously been given a reprimand or final warning, which national research has shown is often the case (YJB, 2003).

We might not expect a low tariff sanction, such as the referral order, to have immediate impacts upon the rates of young people ending up in custody. Nevertheless, the experience of the 1980s showed that even pre-court developments can have impacts further along the sanctioning chain. Despite a recent dip in the numbers of young people in custody in the latter half of 2003, the trend has continued for numbers to rise once more. While this is unlikely to be attributable to referral orders in any direct or indirect way, it does remind us of the general climate within which restorative justice-inspired interventions must operate.

There are questions about the extent to which panel meetings can ever accord fully with restorative justice principles of voluntary participation while they remain firmly located within a penal context, surrounded by various 'coercive sticks', inducements and judicial incentives. Despite the consensual imagery, as this research has shown, some young people may feel they have little choice but to comply with what they are told to do.

Organising youth offender panels presents considerable administrative hurdles that challenge traditional ways of working. Holding panel meetings in the evening and at weekends requires different working patterns; facilitating the attendance of the diverse participants presents difficulties of organisation and timing; and finding appropriate venues challenges the extent to which panels are rooted in local community infrastructures. Moreover, administering panels creatively and flexibly often sits awkwardly within risk-averse professional cultures.

Rotas of community volunteers, for example, are not ideal ways of constituting youth offender panels, but present a rational means of managing them. So, too, does the strategy of scheduling numerous back-to-back panel meetings in one sitting. Nevertheless, these all serve to limit the restorative potential of panels. In practice, balancing the demands of rational management and accommodating the emotional, expressive and human dimensions of restorative justice constitute a fundamental but precarious dynamic in implementing youth offender panels. Under such pressures, there are dangers that panel meetings increasingly become routinised and formalised, losing their creative and flexible party-centred dynamic. Standardised hours of community reparation, pre-packaged activities drawn from a list (like coats off a peg) and standard-term contracts, while understandable, all leave less scope for the deliberative qualities of panels. Finally, the apparent inflexibility of the referral order length and national standards requirement for a minimum amount of contact can mean (particularly in longer orders) that an initial positive response by a young person may become a negative experience.

Hence, it is important that panels adhere to and enhance their restorative justice principles, particularly in the face of pressures towards standardisation. They need to engage constructively with young people, parents and victims and ensure that contracts are the result of negotiation rather than imposition. It is also crucial that panels and the YOS provide the necessary support to ensure that young people and victims are reintegrated into their local communities and not further harmed by the experience of involvement in a referral order.

Nevertheless, referral orders offer youth justice a means of engaging local communities in positive responses to crime, which seek less to stigmatise and exclude young people, but rather to give them a say in how they might make amends and provide them with a stake in addressing the causes of their offending. Youth offender panels afford the opportunity to encourage local dialogue and deliberation about young people and crime, which is more informed and reflective than the media demonisation of young people that currently dominates public debate. They also offer a means of responding to victims in a manner that recognises their needs and expectations. In so doing, the restorative justice principles that inform referral orders reconfigure and open up the way in which youth justice should be thought about and judged, not merely in terms of processing offenders, costs and reconvictions, but also in terms of the experiences of victims, young people and their families, the nature of their community embeddedness and public perceptions of the legitimacy and fairness of local justice. As such, the chair of the YJB may be correct in his recent acknowledgement that referral orders and youth offender panels together may constitute the 'jewel in the youth justice crown' (Morgan, 2005). It is hoped that this report provides some insights into their operation and the manner in which they are experienced, notably with regard to the role and integration of victims, for this complex practical and conceptual issue remains one of their biggest challenges.

References

Biermann, F. and Moulton, A. (2003) *Youth offender panel volunteers in England and Wales, December 2003*, Online report 34/03, London: Home Office.

Bottoms, A.E. (1995) 'The philosophy and politics of punishment and sentencing', in C. Clarkson and R. Morgan (eds) *The politics of sentencing reform*, Oxford: Clarendon.

Braithwaite, J. (1989) *Crime, shame and reintegration*, Cambridge: Cambridge University Press.

Braithwaite, J. and Mugford, S. (1994) 'Conditions of successful reintegration ceremonies: dealing with juvenile offenders', *British Journal of Criminology*, vol 34, no 2, pp 139-71.

Christie, N. (1977) 'Conflicts as property', *British Journal of Criminology*, vol 17, no 1, pp 1-15.

Cohen, S. (1985) *Visions of social control*, Cambridge: Polity Press.

Crawford, A. (2004) 'Involving lay people in criminal justice', *Criminology and Public Policy*, vol 3, no 4, pp 693-702.

Crawford, A. and Enterkin, J. (2001) 'Victim contact work in the Probation Service: paradigm shift or Pandora's box?', *British Journal of Criminology*, vol 41, no 4, pp 707-25.

Crawford, A. and Newburn, T. (2002) 'Recent developments in restorative justice for young people in England and Wales: community participation and representation', *British Journal of Criminology*, vol 42, no 3, pp 476-95.

Crawford, A. and Newburn, T. (2003) *Youth offending and restorative justice*, Cullompton: Willan Publishing.

Daly, K. (2001) 'Conferencing in Australia and New Zealand: variations, research findings and prospects', in A. Morris and G. Maxwell (eds) *Restorative justice for juveniles*, Oxford: Hart Publishing.

Daly, K. (2003) 'Mind the gap: restorative justice in theory and practice', in A. von Hirsch, J. Roberts, A.E. Bottoms, K. Roach and M. Schiff (eds) *Restorative justice and criminal justice: Competing or reconcilable paradigms*, Oxford: Hart Publishing.

Daly, K. and Hayes, H. (2001) 'Restorative justice and conferencing in Australia', in Australian Institute of Criminology, *Trends and Issues in Crime and Criminal Justice*, No 186, February.

Hall, S. (1979) *Drifting into a law and order society*, London: Cobden Trust.

Hayes, H., Prenzler, T. and Wortley, R. (1998) *Making amends: Final evaluation of the Queensland Community conferencing pilot*, Brisbane: Griffith University.

Holdaway, S., Davidson, N., Dignan, J., Hammersley, R., Hine, J. and Marsh, P. (2001) *New strategies to address youth offending: The national evaluation of the pilot youth offending teams*, London: Home Office.

Home Office (1997) *No more excuses*, London: Home Office.

Home Office (2000) *Implementation of referral orders – Draft guidance for youth offending teams*, London: Home Office.

Home Office (2002) *Referral orders and youth offender panels*, London: Home Office/Lord Chancellor's Department /Youth Justice Board.

Home Office (2003a) *Restorative justice: The government's strategy*, London: Home Office.

Home Office (2003b) *Prison statistics for England and Wales, 2002*, Cm 5996, London: Home Office.

Home Office (2003c) *Important changes to referral orders from 18 August 2003*, London: Home Office/Department. for Constitutional Affairs/Youth Justice Board.

Home Office (2005) *Juvenile reconviction: Results from the 2003 cohort*, Online report 08/05, London: Home Office.

Hough, M. and Roberts, J.V. (2004) *Youth crime and youth justice*, Bristol: The Policy Press.

Hoyle, C., Young, R. and Hill, R. (2002) *Proceed with caution: An evaluation of the Thames Valley Police Initiative in Restorative Cautioning*, York: Joseph Rowntree Foundation.

JUSTICE (1998) *Victims in criminal justice*, Report of the Committee on the Role of the Victim in Criminal Justice, London: JUSTICE.

Karp, D. and Drakulich, K. (2004) 'Minor crimes in quaint settings: Practices, outcomes and limits of Vermont Reparative Probation Boards', *Criminology and Public Policy*, vol 3, no 4, pp 655-86.

Marshall, T.F. (1996) 'The evolution of restorative justice in Britain', *European Journal on Criminal Policy and Research*, vol 4, no 4, pp 21-43.

Marshall, T.F. (1999) *Restorative justice: An overview*, London: Home Office.

Marshall, T.F. and Merry, S. (1990) *Crime and accountability: Victim offender mediation in practice*, London: HMSO.

Miers, D., Maguire, M., Goldie, S., Sharpe, K., Hale, C., Netten, A., Uglow, S., Doolin, K., Hallam, A., Enterkin, J. and Newburn, T. (2001) *An exploratory evaluation of restorative justice schemes*, Crime Reduction Research Series Paper 9, London: Home Office.

Morgan, R. (2005) unpublished speech to 'Building on Success: The West Yorkshire YOTs, Five Years on' conference, West Yorkshire Playhouse, Leeds, 20 May.

Morris, A. (2002) 'Critiquing the critics', *British Journal of Criminology*, vol 42, no 3, pp 596-615.

Morris, A. and Maxwell, G. (2000) 'The practice of family group conferences in New Zealand: assessing the place, potential and pitfalls of restorative justice', in A. Crawford and J.S. Goodey (eds) *Integrating a victim perspective within criminal justice*, Aldershot: Ashgate.

Morris, A., Maxwell, G. and Robertson, J.P. (1993) 'Giving victims a voice: a New Zealand experiment', *Howard Journal*, vol 32, no 4, pp 304-21.

Newburn, T., Crawford, A., Earle, R., Goldie, S., Hale, C., Masters, G., Netten, A., Saunders, R., Sharpe, K. and Uglow, S. (2001a) *The introduction of referral orders into the youth justice system*, RDS Occasional Paper No 70, London: Home Office.

Newburn, T., Crawford, A., Earle, R., Goldie, S., Hale, C., Masters, G., Netten, A., Saunders, R., Sharpe, K., Uglow, S. and Campbell, A. (2001b) *The introduction of referral orders into the youth justice system: Second interim report*, RDS Occasional Paper No 73, London: Home Office.

Newburn, T., Crawford, A., Earle, R., Goldie, S., Hale, C., Masters, G., Netten, A., Saunders, R., Hallam, A., Sharpe, K. and Uglow, S. (2002) *The introduction of referral orders into the youth justice system*, HORS 242, London: Home Office.

Page, B., Wake, R. and Ames, A. (2004) *Public confidence in the criminal justice system*, Findings 221, London: Home Office.

Shapland, J. (2000) 'Victims and criminal justice: creating responsible criminal justice agencies' in A. Crawford and J. Goodey (eds) *Integrating a Victim Perspective within Criminal Justice*, Aldershot: Ashgate.

Sherman, L. (2002) Paper presented to the international workshop 'Doing Restorative Justice', University of Keele, 16 July.

Sherman, L.W. and Strang, H., with Woods, D.J. (2003) 'Captains of restorative justice: experience, legitimacy and recidivism by type of offence', in E.G.M. Weitekamp and H.-J. Kerner (eds) *Restorative justice in context*, Cullompton: Willan.

Simmons, J. and Dodd, T. (eds) (2003) *Crime in England and Wales 2002/3*, Statistical Bulletin 07/03, London: Home Office.

Strang, H. (2001) 'Justice for victims of young offenders: the centrality of emotional harm and restoration', in A. Morris and G. Maxwell (eds) *Restorative justice for juveniles*, Oxford: Hart Publishing.

Strang, H. (2002) *Repair or revenge: Victims and restorative justice*, Oxford: Clarendon Press.

Strang, H., Barnes, G., Braithwaite, J. and Sherman, L. (1999) *Experiments in restorative policing: a progress report on the Canberra Reintegrative Shaming Experiments* (RISE), Canberra: ANU.

Tickell, S. and Akester, K. (2004) *Restorative justice: The way ahead*, London: JUSTICE.

Trimboli, L. (2000) *An evaluation of the NSW youth justice conferencing scheme*, New South Wales: Bureau of Crime Statistics and Research.

Tyler, T.R. (1990) *Why people obey the law*, New Haven, NJ: Yale.

Umbreit, M. (1994) *Victim meets offender*, New York, NY: Willow Tree Press.

Van Ness, D. and Strong, K.H. (1997) *Restoring justice*, Cincinnati: Anderson Publishing.

Waterhouse, L., McGhee, J., Loucks, N., Whyte, B. and Kay, H. (1999) *The Evaluation of Children's Hearings in Scotland: Children in Focus*, Social Work Research Findings No 31, Edinburgh: The Scottish Office Central Research Unit.

Wilcox, A. (2004) *The national evaluation of the Youth Justice Board's restorative justice projects*, London: Youth Justice Board (YJB).

YJB (Youth Justice Board) (2003) *Referral orders: Research into the issues raised in the introduction of referral orders into the youth justice system*, London: YJB.

YJB (2004) *Youth justice – annual statistics 2003/04*, London: YJB.

Young, R. (2000) 'Integrating a multi-victim perspective into criminal justice through restorative justice conferences', in A. Crawford and J.S. Goodey (eds) *Integrating a victim perspective within criminal justice*, Aldershot: Ashgate.

Also available from The Policy Press

Youth crime and youth justice
Public opinion in England and Wales
Mike Hough and Julian V. Roberts

This report presents the findings from the
first national, representative survey of
public attitudes to youth crime and youth
justice in England and Wales. It carries clear
policy implications in relation to both public
education and reform of the youth justice
system.

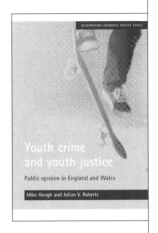

Paperback £14.99 ISBN 1 86134 649 2
245 x 170mm 80 pages November 2004

From dependency to work
**Addressing the multiple needs of
offenders with drug problems**
*Tim McSweeney, Victoria Herrington,
Mike Hough, Paul J. Turnbull and Jim
Parsons*

This report presents the findings from
one of the first evaluations of a British
programme to integrate drug and alcohol
treatment with mental health services, and
education, training and employment support
– the 'From Dependency to Work (D2W)'

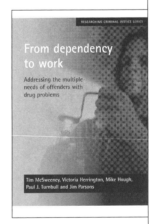

programme. It provides an invaluable insight into the challenges
and difficulties of integrating services in this way and highlights
important lessons for central and regional government on funding
and working with the voluntary sector to deliver services.

Paperback £14.99 ISBN 1 86134 660 3
245 x 170mm 88 pages December 2004

Plural policing
The mixed economy of visible patrols in England and Wales
Adam Crawford, Stuart Lister, Sarah Blackburn and Jonathan Burnett

This timely and important report draws together the findings of an extensive two-year study of developments in the provision of visible policing in England and Wales. Exploring the dynamic relations between different public and private providers, it combines an overview of national developments with a detailed analysis of six focused case studies, including two city centres, one out-of-town shopping centre, an industrial park and two residential areas.

Paperback £14.99 ISBN 1 86134 671 9
245 x 170mm 128 pages March 2005

To order further copies of this publication or any other Policy Press titles please visit **www.policypress.org.uk** or contact:

In the UK and Europe:
Marston Book Services, PO Box 269, Abingdon, Oxon,
OX14 4YN, UK
Tel: +44 (0)1235 465500
Fax: +44 (0)1235 465556
Email: direct.orders@marston.co.uk

In the USA and Canada:
ISBS, 920 NE 58th Street, Suite 300, Portland,
OR 97213-3786, USA
Tel: +1 800 944 6190 (toll free)
Fax: +1 503 280 8832
Email: info@isbs.com

In Australia and New Zealand:
DA Information Services, 648 Whitehorse Road Mitcham,
Victoria 3132, Australia
Tel: +61 (3) 9210 7777
Fax: +61 (3) 9210 7788
E-mail: service@dadirect.com.au

Further information about all of our titles can
be found on our website.